Princeton Theological Monograph Series

Dikran Y. Hadidian

General Editor

23

THE HOLY SPIRIT
IN THE THEOLOGY OF KARL BARTH

The

Holy Spirit

in the

Theology of Karl Barth

by

John Thompson

PICKWICK PUBLICATIONS
Allison Park, Pennsylvania

Published by **Pickwick Publications**
4137 Timberlane Drive
Allison Park, PA 15101-2932
USA

Printed in the United States of America

Library of Congress Cataloging-in-Publication Data

Thompson, John, 1922-
    The Holy Spirit in the theology of Karl Barth / by John
Thompson.
        p.   cm. -- (Princeton theological monograph series ; 23)
    ISBN 0-915138-94-8
    1. Holy Spirit--History of doctrines--20th century. 2. Barth,
Karl, 1886-1968--Contributions in theology of the Holy Spirit.
I. Title.   II. Series.
BT121.2.T48   1991
231'.3'092--dc20
                                        90-23022
                                        CIP

CONTENTS

PREFACE

Eight of the following chapters (One, Four, Eleven excepted) were originally delivered as lectures to undergraduate and post-graduate students. Their aim was and is to give a general introduction to the theology of Karl Barth in the context of his life and work as a whole. An attempt has been made to present the material in a way that can be understood by the student and general reader, yet at the same time may be of assistance to the theologian.

The doctrine of the Holy Spirit in Barth has only recently been dealt with in book form—in the work of P. J. Rosato. Account has been taken and a critique offered here of his work. Since Barth's doctrine is very much at the center of present day theology both in the charismatic and ecumenical movements, his contribution to the debate is particularly relevant and important.

The writer is aware of the fact that to attempt to cover these areas in one volume has its own limitations and disadvantages. Nevertheless he hopes the book will offer a guide to some of Barth's thought and will lead readers to study for themselves the profound and stimulating writing of one of the great theologians of this century.

I am indebted to the Editor, Dikran Y. Hadidian for his continuing help and advice and appreciate the permission of the Editor of "Irish Biblical Studies" to use part of Chapter IV—originally published as an article in that journal.

September, 1989   *John Thompson*
Belfast

CHAPTER ONE

THE WAY OF THE SPIRIT

CRITERIA OF INTERPRETATION

One of the issues that must be faced at the beginning of an exposition of any aspect of Barth's theology is the nature and validity of his whole theological method. It has often been pointed out that a key factor in bringing Barth's own thoughts to clarity on method was his writing of the book on Anselm.[1] While this is true, it should, however, be noted that this exercise simply brought to fruition what had long been germinating in his mind and enabled him to begin and carry out the writing of his monumental *Church Dogmatics*. It is now necessary in more detail to outline and evaluate the principles of interpretation implied in Barth's writings. The essential point can be put in two simple ways.

a) "If I understand what I am trying to do in the *Church Dogmatics*, it is to listen to what Scripture is saying and tell you what I hear".[2]

b) Again it can be formulated in the title of a book on Barth's methodology, *Biblische Denkform in der Dogmatik*[3] (Biblical Thought-Form in the Dogmatics). In other words the text and normative standard of Christian faith and theology is Holy Scripture; Barth claims to have found in it a particular thought-form which determines his whole theology and exposition. It is here too that Anselm comes in, for Barth found in him an approach that confirmed his own. Involved in this are certain important emphases that determine the whole of Barth's approach and can be seen repeatedly at work in the *Church Dogmatics*.

1) The unity of form and content. The form the biblical stories and writings take is determined by their content or message; similarly, our theology, based on these testimonies, should also be conditioned by the same content. This content is God's revelation and reconciliation in Jesus Christ as the fulfillment of Israel's history. The form is *nachdenken*, a thinking as it were of God's thoughts after him. Here a decision of supreme importance in two ways is made by Barth. On the one hand this revelation is focused on Jesus Christ and as such excludes all natural theology. This is so not because humanity's place is minimized at the expense of God and his action, but rather the positive affirmation carries the negative within it. Revelation shows us that only through God is God known. If as sinners we seek to know God by ourselves we end with a false god. On the other hand, while Barth never despised philosophy and took an eclectic attitude towards it, neither it nor any other view can be a pre-understanding which should in any way determine the nature of theology.

2) Since revelation is the revelation of *God* it indicates and conveys God as he is, namely, the triune God. It is God in his being and action who is both the object of faith and the content of our thinking in theology. It is for this reason that Barth puts revelation and the Trinity at the forefront of his *Dogmatics* in what Jüngel has rightly called "a hermeneutical decision of the greatest relevance."[4] In other words this doctrine determines the whole content and structure of theology. Thus, while it is true that Barth's theology represents an unparalleled christological concentration, it is for that very reason also primarily and essentially trinitarian. This can be seen in the way the Trinity re-emerges at particular points in the discussion and especially

as it conditions the whole of the *Church Dogmatics*. It is also for the same reason pneumatological, since the Holy Spirit is the Spirit of the Father and the Son. Yet, as is clearly seen in Barth's treatment of all doctrines (including the Trinity), it is from the center in Christ—and the cross and resurrection in particular—that he begins and continues. The convergence and integration of Trinity, christology and pneumatology is clearly seen in another aspect of Barth's view of our knowledge of God. Our knowledge of him is based on his own self-knowledge and this is another reason why we can only know him as he discloses himself to us. But, before we know him he is an object of knowledge to himself as triune —the Father to the Son, the Son to the Father in the unity of the Holy Spirit. This is the Truth of God in its primary objectivity. But this Truth is revealed in the incarnation, in the God-man, where God, who is always Subject—and remains so even in his self-revelation— gives himself to be known in a secondary objectivity in Jesus Christ. The Subject becomes object in order to be known by us. Further, we are given a share in this knowledge—the truth of God's knowledge of himself—by the Holy Spirit.[5]

3) Closely associated with this is the place Barth gives to the doctrines of election and christology. The triune God is the one who acts, who decides in his own will for us and our salvation. His being and action precede and determine all human life and questioning. God not only lives in the fullness and glory of the divine life, but has decided from all eternity to be the God of humanity and in fact in the man Christ Jesus to be the Mediator between himself and us. Jüngel shows how revelant this is to Barth's whole methodology; we follow in our faith and thinking the God who so acts and chooses for us. Jüngel writes, "the encounter between God and man which owes its origin to the movement of God's being is, according to Barth, first and above all the encounter between the electing God and the

elected man which is fulfilled in Jesus Christ. Thus the existence of the man Jesus confronts us with the hermeneutical problem, both with respect to the understanding of God
as well as with respect to the understanding of the self and
the world: 'At no level or time can we have to do with God
without having also to do with this man. We cannot con-
ceive ourselves and the world without first conceiving this
man with God as the witness of the gracious purpose with
which God willed and created ourselves and the world and
in which we may exist in it and with it.'"[6] Here we see how
Barth underlines the free grace of God in his election of humanity for himself, and the importance of the place of the
humanity of Jesus Christ both for our existence and for that
of the world. God's movement to us which was in his will
from all eternity and is revealed in Jesus Christ in time is
the key to our knowledge of God, of humanity and of the
world. This emphasis both on election and on the centrality
of the humanity of Jesus Christ in our understanding of
God and his revelation has been further underlined and
made explicit by T. F. Torrance: "It is the incarnation, the
concrete reality of God in space and time, that enables
Barth to think out the ontic as well as the cognitive basis
for theological activity."[7] By this he means that Jesus Christ
is not only the God who comes to us but the perfect human
who in obedience and knowledge reflects and witnesses to
the true nature and knowledge of God. God's revelation in
Jesus Christ is the basis in reality, *ordo essendi*, as well as
the way we apprehend God in our thinking, *ordo cognos-
cendi* .

      4) The nature of revelation in Jesus Christ, the econ-
omy of salvation, contains a *ratio*—a rationality within itself. Barth, following Anselm, sees a three-fold *ratio* inherent in the very nature of revelation, a logic of the Word, the
Logos.[8] (a) There is that of Jesus Christ the Word himself;
(b) there is that to which this revelation points—the transcendent rationality of God; and (c) there is that of our con-

cepts and judgments which seek to interpret and in a measure embody this. "Through the noetic *ratio*, theological enquiry penetrates to the ontic or objective *ratio*, but standing behind all and illuminating all is the *ratio* of God, the *ratio veritatis* identical with God's Being, the divine Word consubstantial with the Father."[9]

For Barth all theological activity has nonetheless a provisional character since it is a human pursuit and can and should be subject to correction. At the same time since it stands in a relationship to the biblical revelation it is determined by the activity of God himself in his Word. Set before the biblical text "it must penetrate into the inner *ratio* of the Scriptures and so into the inner logic and form of the Word which it hears, and seeks to articulate it in an orderly manner or *ratio* in our understanding."[10] This means that as faith seeking understanding it will try faithfully to interpret the biblical revelation and will be enabled to do so. However this in no way guarantees or points to an infallibility of doctrine or dogma, but to truth seeking to and, in some measure, corresponding to the Truth of God.

5) Cross, Resurrection and Holy Spirit. Since God reveals himself in Christ as Father, Son and Holy Spirit there is a center, indeed a series of events, from which this can best be expressed. These are the cross, resurrection and pentecost. The deepest humbling of the Son is not just as human but as seen in the contradiction of the cross which is for Barth, paradoxically and miraculously, the highest height and glory of God. Yet the reality and truth in its saving, liberating power would not be known or recognised by us were Jesus not raised. It is the resurrection that reveals the nature of God's act in the crucified and lets it loose on the world. And it is the Holy Spirit accompanying that is effectively God's revelation in us.

For Barth this revelation is always a form of knowledge. This accounts for the fact that some have concluded that for Barth faith is simply knowing we are saved. But knowledge has a depth and varied connotation and is not simply intellectual. It means life, trust and understanding as well as consent of mind and intellectual knowledge, and this comes about only by the power and inspiration of the Holy Spirit. Rosato is right, therefore, in seeing the Holy Spirit as the Spirit of knowledge and understanding. He is generally too keen to make Barth a pneumatic theologian but here his deductions and conclusions can be followed. He sees Barth's methodology, in line with Anselm's, as essentially pneumatic: "Without labelling it such, Barth discovers that Anselm's methodology is pneumatic since its basic presuppositions have the power of God's Spirit as their only possibility; the man of faith, the Christian, is able to reflect on the truth of the creed by means of the inner intelligibility supplied therein. This can be the case solely because the Holy Spirit, God as he grants man faith, also assures faith's reasonableness by illuminating it from within."[11] This is clearly and specifically stated by Barth himself. After discussing the Word as revelation, the witnesses—prophetic and apostolic in Holy Scripture—and the community of faith created by the Word, Barth goes on to speak of the Spirit in relation to our knowledge in theology. He writes, "It is clear that evangelical theology itself can only be pneumatic, spiritual theology. Only in the realm of the power of the Spirit can theology be realized as a humble, free, critical, and happy science of the God of the Gospel. Only in the courageous confidence that the Spirit is the truth does theology simultaneously pose and answer the question about truth."

How does theology become the human logic of the divine Logos? The answer is that it does not *become* this at all; rather, theology may find that the Spirit draws near and comes over it, and that theology may then, without resisting, but also without assuming dominion over the Spirit, simply rejoice and obey its power."[12] Theology becomes unspiritual when it ignores the Spirit or seeks to possess it..

The significance for Barth's pneumatology is clearly seen and stated by Rosato: "In short: the enlightening power which makes both man's faith and its object, God's self-disclosure of his own Truth, verifiable is not the ingenuity of the theologian but the grace of the Holy Spirit ."[13]

This has several implications. In the first place theology is not a mere intellectual exercise but a form of obedient, humble worship beginning on our knees before the Lord and, therefore, is a form of prayer.[14] Secondly, it implies that, since the Holy Spirit alone confirms and verifies the truth of God and its teaching, neither reason nor anything else can be its criterion or judge. We move within a self-enclosed circle in one sense, yet one which opens up to include us by grace and the Spirit giving us participation in the knowledge of the divine life and love. Thirdly, since the Holy Spirit controls us and enables us to interpret the truth of God in Jesus Christ, neither we nor the Church can claim a monopoly of it in our theological statements or that it passes over into our inner spiritual states and is in some way identical with them. T. F. Torrance remarks, "That would imply that the truth of God is identical with the collective subjectivity of the Church or that the Holy Spirit is the immanent soul and mind of the historical church impregnating it with the truth of God. That would imply the identity of dogmas with Dogma."[15] The Spirit guarantees that what we say does, humanly speaking, conform to God's truth but is never as such immediately identical with it as an infallible utterance of a Pope would claim that it is. The Spirit is always the Lord and the interpreter of the truth of God.

What is one to say of this way of doing theology—the Way of the Spirit? Clearly to speak of the Spirit in this connection does not mean that Barth is exclusively pneumatic in the sense that other doctrines are secondary. Rather theology is based on and related to the triune God, to election, to the person and work of Jesus Christ in revelation and reconciliation. To that extent the attempt of Rosato to give Barth a primarily pneumatic slant cannot be followed. Pneumatology is a very important aspect of theology but not the whole of it. It is integrated into and integral to the whole content of the *Church Dogmatics* but is never its primary thrust.

More obvious is the perennial question: can the exclusion of a pre-understanding and of all ways from humanity to God, of natural theology be maintained? Is there not here the danger of having a text without a context and can one indeed understand the meaning of God's Word and will without a prior framework of thought and knowledge by which to judge it? There are two answers which one can give in reply from the perspective of Barth's position, both of which are clear and to many convincing.

a) To make any thought-form or philosophy the criterion or basis of theology endangers and goes contrary to the nature of God's revelation. God cannot be controlled or bound by human thought, or known except in so far as he gives himself to be known. This excludes any pre-understanding determining the method of Christian knowledge. On the other hand to say that the Word cannot be understood save by the Spirit is only half the truth. Barth's position is clearly christological and pneumatic. Since God and humanity are one though distinguished in Jesus Christ, only by the Spirit can this truth be known. At the same time Jesus Christ is truly human and this fact opens the way to, as well as determining the nature of our knowledge of and thinking about, God. Our incapacity to receive the Word of God save by the Spirit has as its correlate the necessity that our minds be redirected by the rational nature of the Word in order to apprehend and interpret it. Theology is thus based on Christ as the Scripture witnesses to him and as the Creeds confess him. Jesus Christ is not only our life through faith but is also the truth and the way to that truth. In other words the revelation in Christ, illumined by the

Spirit, is the basis and way to understanding; but since this is also a human word, it involves the will, mind and thought of human beings penetrating into its inner meaning and structure. Like christology human knowledge of the divine revelation has this divine-human character. This is neither exclusively pneumatic nor rational but, properly understood, both.

b) Barth does not believe we can approach interpretation simply with a *tabula rasa*—a clean sheet. Everyone comes with some pre-understanding, some philosophy explicit or implicit, some thought-form (*Denkschematismus*, as he calls it).[16] It is how this is used that is important. If it is taken to be a way in which the revelation of God in Christ is to be determined and understood then this is to be rejected. Barth indicates, therefore, five attitudes towards philosophy and concepts of ours which he believes should be adopted.

1) Scripture is the witness of apostles and prophets to God's revelation and is primarily understood by the Spirit. No philosophy can take the place of such witnesses, compete with them or properly interpret them. Such a philosophy can participate in a biblical mode of thought but cannot be something that predetermines its interpretation.

2) Our ways of thinking and our presuppositions as they are brought to Scripture can only be in the nature of hypotheses, essays or experiments: "If it becomes serviceable, then it will be in the service and under the control of the Word whose explanation lies in itself."[17]

3) Such a scheme of thought "can claim no independent interest in itself." It can be dangerous if it makes such a claim: "Independent interest can be claimed only by the scriptural mode of thought which takes precedence of ours."[18]

4) No one scheme of thought can claim preference to another. All are contingent and provisional; only the biblical is basic and ultimate.

5) A philosophy can be of service in elucidating the Word if it submits to being itself criticised in the service of the Word, so gaining a legitimate critical power.

In other words all thought schemes or philosophies may be used as servants but not as masters, not as forms which bring an outside frame of reference or criterion to bear on the biblical testimony to divine revelation. The Word through its witnesses, interpreted by the Spirit, yet taking hold of our minds and understanding, re-directing them and our thoughts, is in fact the criterion of theology.[19]

NOTES

1. Karl Barth, *Anselm: Fides Quarens Intellectum*, Anselm's Proof of the Existence of God in the Context of his Theological Scheme; trs. Ian W. Robertson, London: S.C.M., 1960, Reprint, The Pickwick Press, 1975. Very varied interpretations of Anselm have been given. See, for example, John McIntyre, *St. Anselm and his Critics, a re-interpretation of the Cur Deus Homo*, Edinburgh: Oliver and Boyd, 1954. G. Watson, "A Study in St. Anselm's Soteriology and Karl Barth's Theological Method", *Scottish Journal of Theology, (S.J.T.)* Vol. 42. No. 4, 1989, p. 493-513.

2. Quoted by David F. Ford, "Barth's Interpretation of the Bible." in *Karl Barth: Studies of his Theological Methods*, ed. S.W. Sykes, Oxford: Clarendon Press, 1979, p. 55 from R. C. Johnson, 'The Legacy of Karl Barth,' in *Reflection* LXVI, May 1969, New Haven, Conn. p. 4.

3. Wolfhart Schlichting, *Biblische Denkform in Der Dogmatik*, Theologischer Verlag, Zurich, 1971.

4. Eberhard Jüngel, *The Doctrine of the Trinity*, God's Being is in Becoming; trs. Horton Harris, Edinburgh and London: Scottish Academic Press, 1976, p. 4.

5. *Church Dogmatics*, (*C.D.*), II/1, pp. 49ff.

6. Op.cit., p. XXI. The enclosed quotation is from *C.D.*, IV/2, p. 33.

7. T. F. Torrance, *Karl Barth: An Introduction to his Early Theology, 1910-1931*, London: S.C.M., 1962, p. 193.

8. Ibid., pp. 182ff. See Torrance for an admirable summary of Anselm based on an unpublished essay by his brother Professor James B. Torrance (Ibid., p. 10).

9. Ibid., p. 187.

10. Ibid., p. 188.

11. Philip J. Rosato, *The Spirit as Lord. The Pneumatology of Karl Barth*, Edinburgh: T. & T. Clark, 1981 p. 38.

12. Karl Barth, *Evangelical Theology: An Introduction*; trs. Grover Foley, Edinburgh: T & T Clark, 1979, pp. 55-56. Two recent books on the Holy Spirit deserve mention. Alasdair Heron, *The Holy Spirit*, London: Marshall, Morgan Scott, 1983. Tom Smail, *The Giving Gift. The Holy Spirit in Person*, London: Hodder & Stoughton, 1988. Each gives considerable attention to Barth in light of the modern debate. Smail has also summarised Barth's writings on the Holy Spirit in his article, "The Doctrine of the Spirit", *Theology Beyond Christendom*, Essays on the centenary of the birth of Karl Barth, May 10, 1986, ed. John Thompson, Allison Park, Pickwick Publications, 1986, pp. 87-111. Smail is too critical in stating that Barth has "a tendency to subordinate the Spirit to the Son in a one-sided way. . .so that pneumatology is in danger of being merged into Christology" (ibid., p. 108). This is almost exactly the opposite of Rosato's attempt to make Barth chiefly a theologian of the Holy Spirit. Neither is, in our view, correct.

13. Rosato, op cit., pp. 38-39.

14. Barth, *Evangelical Theology*, p. 18.

15. T. F. Torrance, *Theological Science*, Oxford University Press, 1969, pp. 351-352.

16. *C.D.*, I/2, pp. 728ff. For this next section cf., also Walter Kreck, *Grundentscheidungen in Karl Barths Dogmatik*, Neukirchener Verlag, 1978, pp. 175ff, where Kreck lists the same points as Barth's adequate answer to his critics.

17. Ibid., p. 731.

18. Ibid., pp. 730, 731.

19. For a fuller discussion of this whole area see Jean-Louis-Leuba: "Karl Barth et la philosophie. Essai de clarification". *Revue de Théologie et de Philosophie*, Vol. 19, 1987/iv, pp. 473-501.

CHAPTER TWO

REVELATION AND THE TRINITY[1]

A. REVELATION

One of the central questions of the Christian faith is, how do we know God and who is the God whom we know? Barth gives what is for him a characteristic answer that we know God because God has revealed himself to us—only through God is God known. We do not by searching find out God but what neither ear nor heart nor eye of humans can perceive or see God has made known to those who love him. This has clearly two sides, that the true and living God is not unknown or unreachable but has come and opened up his life to us and ours to him, created fellowship between them. Indeed a central theme of Barth's theology is that it is this relationship of God to us and us to God centered and manifest in Jesus Christ that is the Word of God and the true meaning of revelation. The negative is the rejection of all natural theology—for Barth believes that humanity as finite is incapable of the infinite: and, more seriously, that sinful human nature is incapable of perceiving, receiving and conceiving the nature of the true God.[2] What humanity does, as Calvin also said, is to project to infinity it's own conceptions of God, false conceptions at that; it creates a god or gods in its own image. In other words it fashions idols. Now this strong opposition of Barth's to all natural theology is simply because the true knowledge of God given in revelation makes it not only *superfluous* but *impossible*.[3] It is *superfluous* because all that we need to know of God who the true God is—is given here in Jesus Christ. It is impossible because the nature of God as given in the Christian revelation, that is, that a crucified man is the very revelation of the being of God, could never be known otherwise. Neither the traditional proofs of the existence of God nor the Kantian moral imperative lead us in that direction or to that conclusion. Barth writes, "Note well: in the whole Bible of the Old and New Testaments not the slightest attempt is ever made to prove God."[4]

This statement gives us the positive clue to who God is, where he may be known and is known. God is known through the teaching and testimony of Holy Scriptures of both the Old and New Testaments and this is centered and focused in the covenant with Israel and in Jesus Christ the Son of God, the fulfiller of that covenant.[5] Strictly speaking there is only this one revelation in Jesus Christ foretold and foreshadowed in Israel and manifest in God's Son. There is no final revelation, as Niebuhr says, nor is this the crown of revelation as William Temple said,[6] but there is *the* one revelation, the one Word of God, his self-expression, his personal self-giving in Jesus Christ. Again, Barth would probably agree with those who say that revelation is the self-disclosure of the personal God rather than truths about God. Of course, Truth is involved in this self-disclosure and truths are too, but while these propositional types of truth are involved it is primarily, essentially the approach, the coming, the revealing of the living God to us as the Truth in person and for us that is revelation and that is central.[7]

If revelation is God[8] manifest in Jesus Christ the central, focal points of Christ's life are the cross and resurrection. This does not mean that the life of Jesus is unimportant but rather that it is to be understood as divine revelation in the power of the crucified One and in the light of his resurrection. Indeed Barth, while identifying revelation with Jesus Christ as a whole, often speaks of the resurrection and the period of the forty days as the definitive revelation where God is really seen and known as he is.[9] We can, therefore, say that the light the resurrection casts back on the cross, on the whole life of Jesus and on the history of Israel shows all of these, retrospectively, to be revelation. Barth quotes with approval the words of one of the old theologians J. A. Bengel, *Spirant resurrectionem*;[10] they breathe the resurrection.

For Barth, however, the paradox in the divine revelation is that revelation is also a concealing. The *deus revelatus*, the God revealed, is also the *deus absconditus*, the God concealed.[11] God is veiled not only because God is invisible—no one has seen God at any time—but also because in the revelation in Jesus Christ he comes veiled in the flesh. A simple illustration of this is the fact that many in Jesus' day saw only a man; only the eyes of faith opened up by the revelation of the Father saw Jesus as the Messiah, the Son of God.[12] But it is above all on the cross that God is most clearly revealed. Barth writes, "The proper being of the one true God (is) in Jesus Christ the crucified."[13] Here in the greatest possible contradiction God is at one and the same time concealed and yet known as he really is. But it is the resurrection that shows this contradiction, this supreme veiling and this darkest hiddenness to be the revelation of the very nature of the true God himself. It is this death that manifests the life of God, so that, following Barth, some theologians like Moltmann in *The Crucified God* and Jüngel in his book on *The Trinity* speak,[14] as Luther also did, of the crucified God or the death of the living God— phrases that must be carefully used and defined. By this is not meant that God actually ceases to be, which is an impossibility, but that it is by submitting himself in the man Jesus to death, in his union with him on the cross in his atoning death, that the very nature of life, of the living and true God is revealed.

Now there are four things that follow from this conception of revelation.

a) It is God as he really, truly and fully is who is manifest here. There is nothing behind the revealed God yet to be known, but rather God in his revelation is God as he is in himself in all the depths of his deity and to all eternity. Here Barth is speaking against two ideas which occasionally (he believed) crept into the views of the Reformers. One held by Luther[15] was that we only know God as revealed but God in his being is not always God as he is revealed and is not always fully known. Fundamentally Barth agreed with Luther, that theology is a theology of the cross and God is known there, but Luther is ambiguous in places. Barth's other difficulty was with Calvin's doctrine of predestination. Barth believed[16] that Calvin taught much the same as he did, that Christ is the mirror of God's election, but Calvin also taught that this election is not always fully identical with his revelation in Jesus Christ. There is a secret counsel or an absolute decree behind the back of Jesus Christ as it were, and it is here that God decides for or against humanity. Barth is, I believe, right to say that there is no secret depth in God which is different from or other than his revealed will and way in the Son. Here is God's true nature. Revelation reveals the very being of the living God himself. Now this does not mean that God is given into our hands or control, that there is no mystery or majesty in God, but quite the opposite. Nor does it mean that we may fully know him here and now or grasp him wholly by our concepts. But it does mean that the mystery of God's being is that not of an unknown being but of the unutterable love, grace and mercy shown to us in the crucified and risen Lord Jesus Christ.

b) Secondly, God's being in revelation is a being *in action*, again an important and central aspect of Barth's whole theology. God is revealed as a living, dynamic, active God. Revelation has always what Barth calls an *event* character.[17] It happens once for all, not many times but at one point in time for all time and for all humanity in the history of Israel and in the history of Jesus Christ. In this sense it is unrepeatable, though its power and efficacy reach out to all people and all ages.

To put it otherwise, revelation is always reconciliation or atonement. God's revelation reveals not only the truest and deepest depths of God, but the real and abysmal iniquity of humanity and it does so precisely in the conditions of our rebellion, sin and disobedience. God comes not just to speak about himself, but in Christ to be the living, saving God in action bearing his judgment on sin, effectuating salvation, bringing liberation, acting on our behalf. He is *deus pro nobis*, God for us in Jesus Christ. God's being is a being in action on the cross of Christ. It is only as God comes and saves that revelation breaks through the barriers of our pride, sloth, and falsehood separating us from him. So the revelation of God is that of Jesus Christ as the Mediator cleansing from guilt and sin by sin-bearing, accepting judgment and bringing God and humanity together in reconciliation. It is a manifestation of grace, mercy, forgiveness and peace to actual humanity and our world in its alienation and estrangement. Thus God is in revelation in action, in reconciliation or atonement.[18]

c) Thirdly, revelation can be described and is often described by Barth as history, and theology consequently as narration.[19] It is always and quite simply a story that is told, a story of God's being in action in Israel and in its history and in the history of Jesus Christ and of the Church. Revelation takes place in history and as history. To neglect this historical nexus and context is to make the faith a mere philosophy, a mere idea or concept of which Jesus is but the exemplar and illustration with whom one could possibly even, at a pinch, do without. History, however, does not make the Christian faith the act of God; it is not as such revelation, but revelation only comes in and through history. The Gospel is always a story that is told, good news for bad times.

This can be otherwise affirmed by saying that revelation is the unfolding of God's faithfulness to himself, of his own history, his own holy and loving nature, his faithfulness to his covenant with his people, the revelation of his power to effect what he wills despite all our rebellion and all appearances to the contrary. It is the victorious carrying through of God's actual will and election in the particular history of Israel and the covenant, and of Jesus and the new covenant. In fact Barth can also say that as this history reflects the very nature of God, God himself in his inner relations as Father, Son and Holy Spirit has a history and is a history in himself.[20]

d) Fourthly, revelation is the revelation of a God who is always Sovereign and Lord. Barth speaks of God as a being who is indissolubly Subject,[21] who is the sovereign Lord of all. We can never control him, but he is the Lord to whom in our living, action and thinking we are always subject. God is free in the sovereignty and comes to us in grace. No necessity in God or even in our sin compels him to be our Lord and Saviour, but simply the free, gracious election he has made of himself to be the God of humanity and of humanity to be with God.

Consequently the proper response to God's revelation is faith and obedience. Barth quotes with approval Calvin's words that all right knowledge of God is born in obedience.[22] Since God is outside our control but comes and reveals himself in gracious freedom and love the only adequate reaction or response on our part, corresponding to and reflecting his action, is a faith that is obedience and issues in love. In fact this knowledge is not theoretical or simply intellectual mainly, but practical, the personal response of a redeemed person to a personal redeeming God. Again and in consequence theology is an act of worship; it

is essentially prayer; it begins on our knees before the
Lord.[23] It is doxological, acknowledging his majesty in lowliness, his Lordship in service, his divinity in the atoning
cross.

B. REVELATION AND THE TRINITY

One or two preliminary remarks about the Trinity in
Barth's theology are necessary and in order at this point. In
contrast to the majority of theologians he places the Trinity
at the forefront of his *Church Dogmatics*.[24] Others like Peter Lombard in the Middle Ages did the same, but Barth realizes how isolated is his position in so doing. Many confessions of the post-reformation age began with the
Scriptures though quite a number of them began with the
doctrine of God. Barth, however, while basing all his theology on Holy Scripture, nevertheless feels that the Trinity,
which says who the God is who is made known in Christ
through the Scripture, should come first, and this has a basic significance in determining the rest of Church doctrine.
If we can say that God in his very nature is the triune God
then this conditions the rest of our theology and of our
thinking, because the Trinity is primary. According to
Barth, the Trinity is the distinctive Christian idea of God.
He writes, "The doctrine of the Trinity is what basically
distinguishes the Christian doctrine of God as Christian,
and therefore what already distinguishes the Christian concept of revelation as Christian, in contrast to all other possible doctrines of God or concepts of revelation."[25]

In the second place "the doctrine of the Trinity is a
work of the Church,"[26] as indeed is all other doctrine. The
Bible nowhere explicitly states it. It is nevertheless implicit
in Scripture and is a necessary and correct exposition of its
testimony. "This doctrine as such does not stand in the texts
of the Old and New Testament witness to God's revelation.

.. It is exegesis of the texts in the speech ... of a later situation."[27]

In the third place the basis of the Trinity is a *single* basis. It is the biblical revelation. Barth is unique in putting it in this way. He calls this the root of the doctrine of the Trinity.[28] It has this single base and no other. Here Barth differs from the great Augustine[29] to whom he is so similar in many ways and from whom he learned so much. Augustine affirmed that revelation was the prime basis but stated that there were other secondary bases in the structure of nature and of man, the so-called *vestigia trinitatis,* that is, traces of the Trinity;[30] for example, sun, ray, heat, or Augustine's most famous example, one who loves, the thing loved and love itself. All these Barth denies and affirms that there is only one basis in God's action in revelation.

Earlier we saw that revelation is centered in and is identical with Jesus Christ. There is only one revelation. But if that is so, there are nevertheless three aspects of it and these accord with the scriptural witness.[31] The revelation in Jesus Christ is of one who is Lord, who is God; and this points to a Revealer who is the same Lord, the same God, the same subject of revelation. It points also to one who might in one sense be called the person who completes revelation, brings revelation to humanity, involves us in it. This third aspect is God again in another form, the same God, the same Lord; thus we have the one God as the Revealer, the revelation, and this reaching out to and involving humanity, what Barth calls revealedness. The one God in his revelation distinguishes himself from himself not as another God, but as three ways in which the one God exists, comes to us, is known by us and experienced. To put it in more traditional language God reveals himself as the Father through the Son by the Holy Spirit—God above us, God for us and God in and with us. He is God in this unity of being yet in the distinctions of ways of being. Barth emphasises against all anti-Trinitarians that there is no unity except as Trinity.[32] The one true and living God subsists in this unity in these three distinctions within his personal being. God is *one* in three and there is no other unity; but he is also *three* in one. This affirms the fact that God is not alone or lonely in his being, that there are relationships within God himself which must be underlined. If we designate these as "persons" in the modern sense then we are in difficulties since a person is a separate individual consciousness. God is personal of course. Each mode of being, each distinction in the divine being is personal, but not separate, else we end up with tritheism. Barth prefers to follow an ancient tradition and takes *mode of being*[33] instead of person, to distinguish the three ways in which God exists. Either is acceptable so long as we know what we are talking about and so long as we do not deny either the distinctions or the one personal being of God.

Another way of stating the doctrine of the Trinity is to say that God repeats himself three times, yet each is a distinct and distinctive way in which he exists. God does not become someone or something else or divide himself up. Two qualifications must be made to this. Each distinct way of God's being coinheres, interpenetrates the other—this is known as *perichoresis*. When the triune God acts *ad extra*, towards us, these actions are one, the *opera trinitatis ad extra sunt indivisa*, the external works of the Trinity are indivisible.

How do we know all this about the internal and external being and works of God? Is a great deal of this not speculation? Barth has a central and definitive answer, namely, what God is in himself is known from what he is and does in revelation. It has sometimes been put like this—the economic Trinity, that is, what God is in the economy of salvation in the world for us, he is as such in himself. There is no other way of knowing who God is. This is the way God has made known, but this way is fully adequate and wholly reliable as we find it in the biblical

testimony. The economic Trinity is the way to what is
known as the immanent Trinity, how God is in himself.[34]

If in this light we look at each aspect in turn,[35] at
each "person" or mode of being, then we speak first of God
as the Revealer or as the Father. It is sometimes said (and
Barth accepts this) that the Father is the fount and origin of
the whole deity. At any rate he is the one from whom the
Son comes and has his personal existence eternally. In this
light the Father is known as the source of all being outside
himself as well as within the deity. He is the Lord of our
existence and of all things, one from whom they and we
come; we owe our existence completely to him. As the Father is the source of the Son, so he is of all things. What is
therefore most proper to the Father is creation. Hence the
doctrine of what is known as appropriation, that is, the
work most appropriate to each person. Secondly, in Jesus
Christ we have the Reconciler, the one who alone of the
three was incarnate. This again is the designation appropriate to what God has done in revelation. It would be both
wrong and inappropriate to speak of the Father or the Holy
Spirit as becoming incarnate, no matter how much we
speak of all being involved in this action. The center of the
revealing activity of God is in the Son. Thirdly, the work
appropriate to the third mode of God's being is called by
Barth redemption and by this he means ultimate salvation
at the end of time. It has however, both a present and a future dimension. The Spirit is the Lord who brings us
Christ's reconciliation, sets us free, makes us children of
God, but at the same time is the firstfruits and pledge of future redemption; so the appropriate work of the Spirit is this
form of salvation. Therefore, while each person or mode of
being has an appropriate function and work, each at the
same time participates in the activities of the others. Their
works are indivisible. The Son is only Son with the Father,
and Son and Father are only such in the unity of the Holy
Spirit. The Son is with the Father, the agent of creation just

as the Father and the Holy Spirit cannot be dissociated from the Son in the work of reconciliation. Hence pneumatology is related to a strictly christocentric view of revelation.

In his later thinking on the Trinity Barth adds several further thoughts. Four of these deserve mention.

a) That there is an above and a below in God,[36] a giving and a receiving, a commanding and an obedience but all in love, for God is love. All this is true without in any way injuring or querying the unity and equality of God in the three modes of being. There is in a sense therefore a humility in God, which is the basis and possibility of the self-humbling in the Son to earth.

b) There is a dynamic movement in God[37] who is never to be conceived in static terms. The older theologians did not give much place to this but it is implicit in their teaching. God is life, movement and relationship, fellowship and love as such in himself and this he communicates to us as Father by the Son and in the Spirit. The love of God, the grace of Christ and the fellowship of the Spirit are God in action for our good and salvation, creating and communicating his own fellowship to us and exalting us to participation in the divine life, communion and love.

c) Since God is Father, Son and Holy Spirit, and comes as incarnate in the Son the Father shares in the passion of Christ.[38] Barth has stimulated modern theology not to repeat the heresy of patripassianism, that is, that the Father suffered, but to see the grain of truth in this—that you cannot have a loving, suffering, dying Son and Saviour without a Father who is involved and shares in some measure in this. The Greek conception of God was connected with the idea of *apatheia*. God could not suffer, but the creature did and Jesus did. This created a form of dualism between God and humanity since if God cannot suffer, how can he become incarnate in the Son? But it also implied a form of dualism between the Father and the Son, one which Moltmann is in danger of repeating in his doctrine of the

Crucified God.[39] Moltmann states that God is against God,
Father against Son on the cross as witnessed by the cry of
dereliction. Yet this contradiction within God in his self-
giving as Father and self-surrender as Son to abandonment
by the Father does not mean the end of God. In a real sense
it is at the same time the expression of their unity in the
power of the Holy Spirit. The suspicion remains that in
Moltmann's view the contradiction in God is not resolved.
Though Moltmann is indebted to Barth for introducing him
to thinking along these lines his solution is less satisfactory
than Barth's. Barth underlines the fact that it is in the supreme opposition to God, in the contradiction of our sin on
the cross that we know the highest height and true nature of
God. God is self-giving love in reconciliation as he overcomes the contradiction in humanity and the very real
threat posed to himself. He writes, "God gives himself, but
he does not give himself away. He does not give up being
God. . . He does not come into conflict with himself. . . .He
acts as Lord over this contradiction even as he subjects
himself to it."[40] So "what he is and does he is and does in
full unity with himself."[41] Modern theology has followed on
in the wake of Barth with this new emphasis on the involvement of God in human suffering and the involvement
of the Father in that of the Son.

        d) Finally, as we have already seen, another way in
which Barth has stimulated thought on the Trinity is by relating it to the cross. Here in the death of the Son, God does
not die, but through acceptance of death and its curse and
judgment on our behalf, he has declared and shown his victorious life and power, his very nature and has too, by the
eternal spirit, offered himself. It is therefore from the cross
and resurrection that one knows who God is and that one is
learning today to define God as Father, Son and Holy Spirit.

C. THE HOLY SPIRIT AND THE TRINITY

When one examines briefly Barth's teaching on the Holy Spirit in relation to the triune God several aspects of it may be elucidated.

The Divinity of the Spirit.[42]

Barth brings forward four main lines of argument:

a) Equality. There are some scriptural passages where the Spirit is implicitly spoken of as in no way inferior to but equal with God, 2 Cor. 3:17; Acts 5:3ff; Mark 3:28ff.

b) Revelation. The affirmation of the deity of the Spirit is better grounded in the reality of God's revelation. The Spirit is a form of that revelation. As we have seen, the Spirit is God in us opening up our lives to know his Word in Jesus Christ and bringing that effectively to us. The Spirit is both the subjective reality and agent of divine revelation.

c) Eschatology. In Barth's view the Holy Spirit points us to the future redemption, is an anticipation of that redemption to which we move and for which we are set free. The Spirit is the source and power of our hope impelling us forward as the first-fruits and foretaste of eternal salvation. To have this promise and awareness, to know this hope is something done for us and in us by God alone.

d) Doxology. With the Father and the Son together the Spirit is worshipped and glorified, as the Nicene Creed says. The Christian community not only worships Father and Son, but at the same time and in the same way the Holy Spirit, thus recognising its divinity.

In all these ways Barth is underlining the affirmation of the biblical testimony to the Holy Spirit as divine.

The Holy Spirit thus comes to us as the Lord. Were

the Spirit not divine but a creaturely manifestation we
would meet it as we do other creatures, have a reciprocal
relationship with it and cooperate with it. As in Roman Catholicism we would be to some extent active subjects in our
own salvation. But this would be to deny that Lordship by
which the Spirit comes actively to challenge our sinful autonomy and subdue our stubborn wills to conform to the divine. We, therefore, meet the Holy Spirit as Lord in the
same way as Father and Son are Lord. The Lordship of the
Spirit is not different from that of the Father and the Son.

The Holy Spirit in relation to Father and Son.[43]

          Barth follows Augustine closely here as in so much
else and speaks of the Holy Spirit as the union and communion of Father and Son, yet at the same time as a distinct
person. How does one know this? Again one can only draw
on the economy of salvation. The Holy Spirit is the bond of
union between God and humanity in Jesus Christ and between Christ and humanity and these unions in turn reflect
how God is in himself. The Holy Spirit is thus a person in
the union and communion of the divine life in the divine
and holy love.
          There are various important insights which are in-
volved in the above statements. In the first place a clear
correspondence between God's being and action in himself
and what he does for us *ad extra* is emphasised. It is this
that is the basis of Barth's emphasis on analogy so clearly
implied in the whole thrust of the *Church Dogmatics*. At
the same time it is a correspondence God alone creates by
his action in Christ through the Holy Spirit; in other words
it is no *analogia entis* (analogy of being) but an *analogia fidei* (analogy of faith).
          In the second place the character of God's action for
humanity indicates clearly the character of God and the
place of the Spirit in the relationship of the persons within

the divine being. This is variously stated by Barth. The central emphasis is that of the Spirit as the mutual self-giving and impartation of Father to Son and Son to Father. It is the same Holy Spirit who enables and creates communion between God and humanity. This communion shows both the reality of our participation in revelation and is indicative of the place of the Spirit in the divine life. Since God and humanity are related to one another and we share in divine revelation by the Holy Spirit this reflects the reality of God's being as participation, sharing, mutual self-giving of Father and Son by the Holy Spirit. "This togetherness or communion of the Father and the Son is the Holy Spirit. The specific element in the divine mode of being of the Holy Spirit thus consists, paradoxically enough, in the fact that he is the common factor in the mode of being of God the Father and that of God the Son. He is what is common to them, not in so far as they are the one God, but in so far as they are the Father and the Son."[44] By this common factor Barth clearly means mutual communion. "He is the act in which the Father is the Father of the Son . . . and the Son is the Son of the Father."[45] In other words in this way he is the triune God. This is the truth and reality our communion in the Spirit attests and affirms.

In the third place this gives truth and certainty to our reconciliation with God. We are in fellowship with and dependent on no creaturely form or reality but on the truth of the being and action of the triune God. Thus the actions "in which he wills to be our God have their basis and prototype in his own essence, in his own being as God."[46] So deep and sure is our union and communion with God by the Holy Spirit. Without this mutual relationship God would not be triune, would not be God and without this our fellowship with God would have no sure foundation. And though this is a movement in God it is one to us and in us because it is first true of God before we participate in it. It is thus this sure foundation that gives us a certain hope. To deny this would be to rob our faith of objective reality and content.

In the fourth place the reality of the Holy Spirit as the union and communion of Father and Son negate all loneliness in God. God is love in this mutuality, indwelling and relationship of Father, Son and Holy Spirit and the Spirit is the bond of love and communion. God is indeed singular and simple, one in being and action, but not an undifferentiated or unstructured unity. He is one in communion. Barth is not kindly disposed to a "Social" Trinity of the Eastern or Anglican type but he affirms a divine fellowship which is the basis and possibility of our union with God and with one another. "As he is the Father who begets the Son he brings forth the Spirit of love, for as he begets the Son, God already negates in himself, from eternity, in his absolute simplicity, all loneliness, self-containment, or self-isolation. Also and precisely in himself, from eternity, in his absolute simplicity, God is orientated to the Other, does not will to be without the Other, will have himself only as he has himself with the Other and indeed in the Other. He is the Father of the Son in such a way that with the Son he brings forth the Spirit, love, and is himself the Spirit, love."[47] Because God is this self-giving Love yet goes out of himself to us the Spirit is both the bond of love between the Father and the Son, between God and humanity and the reality of our fellowship with God. It is the Spirit who draws us out of our sinful isolation and loneliness into the fellowship and love of the triune God.

In the fifth place for Barth the Holy Spirit, while coming into our lives, changing them and bringing us into union with the triune God, remains at the same time Lord over us. The Spirit is both transcendent and immanent, is never to be identified with our spirits or even with our spirituality. The Spirit is always the Lord of our experience of it while creating that experience. Barth writes, "The Holy Spirit, in distinction from all created spirits, is the Spirit who is and remains and always becomes anew transcendent over man even when immanent in him."[48]

A final implication for Barth is that it is only as triune that God is ours. Since the Holy Spirit brings God to us and leads us to know him, the Spirit also makes known to us that from all eternity God is *our* God. He is such as triune and is so to speak "ours in advance". It is precisely as three in one that God is *our* God. As Jüngel points out it is in this way that God is *extra nos, pro nobis,* that is, outside of us and yet for us and so is love. He loved us before we were, "And this Lord can be our God. He can meet us and unite himself to us, because he is God in his three modes of being as Father, Son and Spirit, because creation, reconciliation and redemption, the whole being, speech and action in which he wills to be our God have their basis and prototype in his own essence, in his own being as God. As Father, Son and Spirit God is, so to speak, ours in advance."[49] It is because he is not only Father and Son but also Spirit who brings us into union with God that he is in fact such. It is the Holy Spirlt who both unites the Father and Son and brings us into that same union.

The Holy Spirit and the Filioque.

The *Filioque*[50] is the Western teaching that the Holy Spirit is the Spirit of both the Father and the Son (*Filioque*—and from the Son), and proceeds from both. Orthodoxy teaches, as in the Nicene Creed, that the Spirit comes from the Father alone. One can possibly add that the Spirit comes through the Son, but to say also "from the Son'" is to endanger the place of the Father as the sole source of the deity, that is of both Son and Spirit.

The basis for Barth's acceptance of the *Filioque* and rejection of the Eastern Orthodox position is the correspondence between God's economic and immanent being and activity. To fail to ground the Spirit in the relationship of

Father and Son, as coming from both and as the union of both, would result in a twofold error. First, it would mean a real difference between God in his revelation and God as he is antecedently in himself. Since the Spirit comes from the Father *and* the Son in the economy of salvation it does so eternally in the life of God. Again it would mean that the basis of our faith in God would be evacuated of real content. The reality of our communion with God by the Spirit of Christ and a knowledge of this points to a divine, eternal truth which is endangered in a failure to affirm the *Filioque*. There is thus both a formal and a material weakness in the Eastern position. "The *Filioque* expresses recognition of the communion between the Father and the Son. The Holy Spirit is the love which is the essence of the relation between these two modes of being of God. And recognition of this communion is no other than recognition of the basis and confirmation of the communion between God and man as a divine, eternal truth, created in revelation by the Holy Spirit. The intra-divine two-sided fellowship of the Spirit, which proceeds from the Father and the Son, is the basis of the fact that there is in revelation a fellowship in which not only is God there for man but in very truth—this is the *donum Spiritus sancti*—man is also there for God."[51] Here we see clearly that Barth's position in relation to the nature of revelation and its implications for the Trinity lead him correctly to a doctrine of the Holy Spirit which affirms and defends the *Filioque*. Rosato is right in stating "most interesting, however, is the fact that Barth sees the urgent need to assert God's correspondence to himself precisely when he is developing his pneumatology."[52] This, while true, should not mislead us to think that pneumatology is Barth's main theme in his theology. His whole theology is, as we have seen, trinitarian pursued and viewed from a christological center.

The *Filioque* in Ecumenical Perspective.[53]

Recent debate in the ecumenical movement has raised again in acute form how far the later addition of the *Filioque* to the Niceno-Constantinopolitan Creed (381) was theologically justified. From the point of view of a conciliar decision of the ecumenical church it cannot be justified. Opinion too has changed among many Western theologians who see the *Filioque* as not necessary theologically or, at any rate, requiring considerable modification to make it acceptable. Some of the arguments run as follows. The West generally begins with the unity of God and proceeds to try and fit the Trinity into this unitary view. The result is that the "persons" of the triune God are overshadowed by the unity resulting in a form of Modalism, or semi-Sabellianism. There may be some truth in this since traditional theology made a distinction between the *De Deo Uno* (concerning the one God) and the *De Deo Trino* (concerning the triune God). In so far as a view of God's unity was presupposed in the Western doctrine of the Trinity prior to thinking of the threeness this is a danger. The result is that some Western theologians (Jürgen Moltmann, prominent among them)[54] largely influenced by Eastern thought have been highly critical of the Western view and would be prepared to consider omitting the *Filioque* from the Creed. Underlying this ecumenical concern for greater unity is the theological one for better doctrine. This is combined with a practical desire for a greater awareness of the place of the Trinity in doxology and worship.

While Barth is strongly supportive of the Western approach he does not begin, as much of its tradition does with a prior philosophical conception of God which Easterners so dislike. Instead he and the Easterners have this in-common that both relate the Trinity immediately to Christian revelation, faith, life and worship. Again Barth strongly underlines an Eastern emphasis in his view of the being of God as a being in action similar to the divine *ener-geia*. Moreover, at one point he can say that while the economic Trinity is intelligible to our conception, God in himself as Father, Son and Holy Spirit is beyond our understanding—essentially a mystery. This is similar to the Eastern view of God being unknowable save in the *energeia*. At the same time while Barth held the moderate Orthodox view of Bolotov as reasonable, it was still unacceptable since it did not retain what is basic, namely, the correspondence of economic and immanent Trinity. The same must also be said of the World Council of Churches' statement and suggestions; and of Moltmann's recent book.[55]

Acceptance of the recent thesis for suspension of or dispensing with the *Filioque* is made dependent on the highly dubious view that, since the Spirit was active not only as the One who comes from Christ but in the birth, life and death of Jesus, therefore one can posit a reciprocity between Son and Spirit rather than limiting the Spirit exclusively to Christ in the completed act of reconciliation.[56] This however fails to make a distinction between the Spirit indwelling the human Jesus and its function as the One who makes revelation known and real to humanity as a result of Christ's total being and work. Christ receives the Spirit as human; one cannot speak of the eternal Son of the Father as at any time without the Spirit but only as God with the Spirit. This is not meant to divide the person of the God-man but to point to a necessary distinction in the role of the Spirit in relation to Jesus as human and in relation to the total Christ event which makes a real reciprocity unlikely.

A more fruitful emphasis is that of T. F. Torrance[57] who has spoken of the possibility of a theological-ecumenical consensus along quite different lines, namely the relevance of Barth to Orthodoxy and the more recent approximation of Karl Rahner's[58] views and Barth's.

Rosato rightly sees Barth's emphasis on the correspondence of economic and immanent Trinity and the Spirit as Lord of Christian experience as countering a tendency in Bultmann and Schleiermacher to separate the Spirit from the divine Word and the economic from the immanent Trinity. He writes, "Barth in effect departs from Neo-Protestantism and Christian Existentialism and joins himself to Catholic and Reformational teaching on the Trinity, but he does so in such a way as to link God's essence and God's activity in history much more closely than had been done before."[59]

The conclusion one must reach here is that Western thought, both Roman Catholic and Protestant, follows a similar line with variations in detail. It has basically a common view of the Trinity. The East, however, in its most distinctive writers has a very different conception of the place of the Holy Spirit within the Trinity and possibly of the Trinity itself. Despite, therefore, recent ecumenical meetings and an attempt to have some common ground on this important issue, the differences remain and consensus is not yet forthcoming.

The Holy Spirit, Election and the Trinity.

The basis of the Holy Spirit's work in humanity and the world is, as we have seen, in the triune God. The divine being is however, according to Barth, a being in becoming—in action. God not only moves and is dynamic within himself, but by an eternal decision of his will, has determined to move towards humanity and the world, to be the God of humanity and to make it the covenant partner. In the divine election God has decided in Christ for us and the Holy Spirit's work in time is seen as based on this eternal act.

Election is for Barth the sum of the Gospel,[60] the best of all God's words and works, that God elects humanity to be his and so reveals it as a predestination of himself and his will to be gracious. It is centered in Jesus Christ as electing God and elected man but involves the Father and Holy Spirit also. The Father elects to establish a covenant with humanity, the Son to be obedient to that will and the Holy Spirit resolves to maintain the unity of Father and Son in this action, confirming and demonstrating the Father's offering and the self-offering of the Son. "In the beginning it was the resolve of the Holy Spirit that the unity of God, of Father and Son would not be disturbed or rent by this covenant with man, but that it should be made the more glorious, the deity of God, the divinity of his love and freedom, being confirmed and demonstrated by this offering of the Father and this self-offering of the Son."[61] But since the Son was obedient to the Father the Spirit is the Spirit of this obedience.[62] At the same time the Spirit empowers the human Jesus to fulfil that obedience on earth and so carry out the Father's will. On this basis the Spirit brings us to faith and is its new creative power. The Christian faith has this sure foundation in election and the Spirit has this distinctive function therein.

Barth can go as far as to speak of the pre-existing God-man and of humanity pre-existing also in the Spirit.[63] He does not mean by this that humanity as temporal has, like the Son, an eternal pre-existence. Rather in this way he points to the fact that in the eternal election of the Father and the Son by the Spirit humanity is already intended and included in the divine will and grace. The twin bases of our existence as human and as Christian are the being and action of the triune God and the will of this God in his eternal election in Christ by the Holy Spirit.

This election is centered in Christ but the Holy Spirit has a place too. The Spirit guarantees that the eternal divine resolve effectuated in Christ reaches us, that humanity is incorporated into Christ and shares the divine grace and love. Thus what is ontically real in Jesus Christ in his eternal election becomes noetically present in incarnation and reconciliation and gains entrance into humanity in time by the Holy Spirit. While Jesus Christ is central the Holy Spirit plays an indispensable role. Barth could, however, scarcely affirm Rosato's way of putting it when he writes, "In the Christian that takes place which once took place in Jesus Christ: a Spirit-filled man emerges who gives witness to his brothers concerning the endless glory and goodness of God."[64] This comes dangerously close to saying that Jesus is only a Spirit-filled man and that our Christian lives are simply a repetition of his. This is a half-truth which affirms that the Son of God was as human filled with the Spirit but to take the Spirit-filled aspects as the main truth or almost the whole truth is a very one-sided emphasis.

Rosato is, however, right in his further observation that Barth's view of our salvation is based on the divine election and the inclusive, universal nature of reconciliation.[65] In this respect it is a counter to the nineteenth century subjectivism and individualism represented by Schleiermacher. Our subjective apprehension of our election in Christ is, however, not a human possibility, not simply a pious awareness, in no way our doing, but the work of the Holy Spirit. Rosato writes, "By welding pneumatology to christology, Barth removes even from the subjective appropriation of the Christ event by the believer every trace of subjectivism. . .The strict christological framework in which Barth situates his pneumatology in the *Church Dogmatics* is proof enough that he is struggling against subjectivism with as much force as he can assemble."[66] This Rosato rightly relates to God's eternal election in Jesus Christ.

One could sum up Barth's teaching on the relationship of the Trinity, election and the Spirit in this way. While the Son is the content of the divine election he acts in obedience to the will of the Father and becomes in time what he also eternally wills to be, namely, the God of humanity, the God-man. The Holy Spirit is both the guarantee of the unity of God in the triune life and in his eternal choice. At the same time the Spirit confirms and demonstrates the deity and freedom of God in his action. It is a divine work that the Spirit performs. The self-offering of the Son in obedience to the Father takes shape in time by the same Holy Spirit's agency through the incarnation and by the creation of faith in Christ. God as the triune God is revealed in Christ's action and election by the Holy Spirit. Already in the divine life there is an *opus internum ad extra*—an element in God and his election which envisages humanity and our salvation. God at one and the same time is both *extra nos-pro nobis*. The whole direction and action of the divine being and life is to be the God of humanity, our God in Christ by the Holy Spirit.

These trinitarian and election bases come naturally at the beginning of any interpretation of Barth's pneumatology since they both determine all that follows as source and power of it and re-appear in distinctive ways at various points in the *Church Dogmatics*.

NOTES

1. *Church Dogmatics (C.D.)* , I/1, pp. 295ff.

2. Ibid., pp. 220-221.

3. *C.D.*, II/1, p. 85: "a 'natural' theology is quite impossible within the Church" (ibid.)

4. Karl Barth, *Dogmatics in Outline*, trs. G.T. Thomson, London: S.C.M., 1949, p. 37.

5. *C.D.*, IV/1, pp. 22ff.

6. See H. Hartwell, *The Theology of Karl Barth: An Introduction*, London: Duckworth, 1964, p. 70f for this statement.

7. *C.D.*, I/1, p. 304. Barth follows Calvin by saying revelation is *Dei loquentis persona*—the person of God speaking.

8. *C.D.*, IV/1, pp. 178ff.

9. Ibid., pp. 299ff.

Revelation and the Trinity

10. *C.D.*, IV/2, p. 132.

11. *C.D.*, I/1, pp. 320ff.

12. St Matthew 16:17.

13. *C.D.*, IV/1, p. 199.

14. Jürgen Moltmann, *The Crucified God*, trs. R. A. Wilson and John Bowden, London, S.C.M., 1976, pp. 211ff. Eberhard Jüngel, *The Doctrine of the Trinity*, trs. Horton Harris, Edinburgh and London: Scottish Academic Press, 1976, pp. 83ff.

15. *C.D.*, II/1, p. 210. "In the revelation of God there is no hidden God, no *Deus absconditus*, at the back of his revelation. . . It may often look like this in certain contexts in Luther" (ibid).

16. *C.D.*, II/2, pp. 110-111.

17. *C.D.*, I/1, pp. 88ff. p. 109f.

18. See *C.D.*, IV/1 - IV/3. see especially *C.D.*, IV/1, pp. 157-283.

19. Cf. *C.D.*, II/2, pp. 8ff., *C.D.*, III/1, pp. 81ff. *C.D.*, IV/1, pp. 320ff. This aspect of Barth is discussed by David F. Ford in his essay "Barth's Interpretation of the Bible" in *Karl Barth—Studies of his Theological Methods*, ed. S.W. Sykes, Oxford: Clarendon Press, 1979, pp. 55-87.

20. *C.D.*, IV/1, p. 203f.

21. *C.D.*, I/1, p. 381. *C.D.*, II/1, pp. 10ff.

22 Karl Barth, *Evangelical Theology: An Introduction*, trs. Grover Foley, London: Collins, 1965, p. 22.

23. Ibid., pp. 148-158.

24. *C.D.*, I/1, p. 300. There has been a recent revival in writings on the Trinity particularly in relation to salvation, worship and social and political issues. A good introduction to this debate with an extensive bibliography is *The Forgotten Trinity. The Report of the BCC Study Commission on Trinitarian Doctrine Today*, London: The British Council of Churches, 1989. For a good summary of Barth's earlier work see Claude Welch, *The Trinity in Contemporary Theology*, London: S.C.M. 1964, pp. 13-32. A further treatment of Barth's doctrine in relation to reconciliation is John Thompson, On the Trinity, *Theology Beyond Christendom*, ed., John Thompson, Allison Park, Pickwick Publications, 1986, pp. 13-32.

25. Ibid., p. 301.

26. Ibid., p. 308.

27. Ibid., p. 375.

28. Ibid., p. 304. cf. p. 311. cf. Welch, op.cit., p. 180f.

29. Ibid., p. 334f.

30. Ibid., pp. 333ff.

31. Ibld., pp. 314ff.

32. Ibid., pp. 348ff.

33. Ibid., p. 355f.

34. Ibid., pp. 332 & 479. A powerful defense of Barth and a critique of other modern writers (Moltmann, Pannenberg & Jüngel) is found in Paul D. Molnar, "The Function of the Immanent Trinity in the Theology of Karl Barth", *S.J.T.* Vol. 43. No. 3, 1989, pp. 341-367.

35. Ibid., pp. 384ff.

36. *C.D.*, IV/1, pp. 185ff.

37. *C.D.*, I/1, pp. 393-394.

38. *C.D.*, IV/2, p. 357. Cf. also IV/2, pp. 84-85.

39. Jürgen Moltmann, op. cit., pp. 235ff; see also J. Moltmann, *The Trinity and the Kingdom of God*, trs. Margaret Kohl, London: S.C.M., 1981, pp. 80ff.

40. *C.D.*, IV/1, p. 185.

41. Ibid., p. 186.

42. *C.D.*, I/1, pp. 448ff.

43. Ibid., pp. 469ff.

44. Ibid., p. 469.

45. Ibid., p. 470.

46. Ibid., p. 383.

47. Ibid., p. 483. Eastern thought, much studied today, is close to the "social" view of the Trinity. Cf. John D. Zizioulas, *Being as Communion*, New York: St. Vladimir's Seminary Press, 1985; T. F. Torrance, *The Mediation of Christ.*, Exeter: The Paternoster Press, 1983, p. 59, though a Western theologian speaks of the Trinity in terms of onto-relations. Torrance's large book, *The Trinitarian Faith* is strongly influenced by Eastern patristic thought. A strong defense of the social theory appears in *Trinity, Incarnation and Atonement, Philosophical and Theological Essays,* eds. Ronald J. Feenstra and Cornelius Plantinga Jnr, Notre Dame Press, 1989. Plantinga, "Social Trinity and Tritheism" (ibid. pp. 21-47) and David Brown, "Trinitarian Personhood and Individuality", (ibid., pp. 48-78) are the two contributors.

48. Ibid., p. 488.

49. Ibid., p. 383. Eberhard Jüngel, *The Doctrine of the Trinity*, trs. Horton Harris, Edinburgh and London: Scottish Academic Press, 1976, p. 25.

50. Ibid., pp. 477ff.

51. Ibid., p. 480.

52. Rosato, *The Spirit as Lord*, p. 61.

53. For the recent debate see: *Spirit of God, Spirit of Christ, Ecumenical Reflections on the Filioque Controversy*, ed. Lukas Vischer, London: S.P.C.K., Geneva, World Council of Churches, 1981, Faith and Order Paper No. 103; Alasdair Heron, "The Filioque Clause," in *One God in Trinity*, ed. Peter Toon and James Spiceland, London: Samuel Bagster, 1980, pp.62-67; John Thompson,"The Holy Spirit and the Trinity in Ecumenical Perspective," *The Irish Theological Quarterly*, XXIV, 1980. *The Forgotten Trinity, B.C.C.*, 1989.

54. Moltmann, "Theological Propoals Towards the Resolution of the Filioque Controversy," in *Spirit of God. Spirit of Christ*, pp. 164ff. The B.C.C. Report recommends such an omission. Op.cit., p. 34.

55. Moltmann, *The Trinity and the Kingdom of God*, pp. 178ff.

56. Lukas Vischer, op.cit., pp. 9-10, 18.

57. T. F. Torrance, "Towards an Ecumenical Consensus on the Trinity," *Theologische Zeitschrift*, XXXI, No. 6, pp. 337-350.

58. Karl Rahner, *The Trinity*, trs. Joseph Donceel, London: Burns and Oates, 1979.

59. Rosato, op.cit., p. 59.

60. *C.D.*, II/2, p. 3.

61. Ibid., pp. 101-102.

62. Ibid., p. 106.

63. Ibid., p. 110 speaks of "the pre-existing God-man" "pre-existing" being strangely omitted in the English translation. For the second view see *C.D.*, III/1, p. 56. "We may say in a word that it is in God the Holy Spirit that the creature as such pre-exists."

64. Rosato, op.cit., p. 83.

65. Ibid., p. 83.

66. Ibid., p. 84.

CHAPTER THREE

THE HOLY SPIRIT
AND THE INCARNATION

A. THE INCARNATION

We have already noted that at each stage of the *Church Dogmatics* the doctrine of the Trinity is either implicit or explicitly stated. This is in accord with Barth's hermeneutical procedure of giving it prior place in doctrine. Here in his writing on the incarnation this is clear. While it is the Son alone who becomes incarnate he does so by the will of the Father and through the Holy Spirit. It is thus an act of God in his divine omnipotence, grace and wisdom. Yet, while this is true, it is significant also that the Holy Spirit is the divine mode of being most explicitly mentioned here with the Son. The chief point to underline therefore is that since the Spirit is the unity of the Father and the Son in the Godhead it is also the unity of God and humanity in Jesus Christ. In the incarnation we have true God and true humanity in one. "The incarnation of the Word is a new divine beginning; grace, but grace of the free God; freedom, but freedom of the gracious God. Therefore there is indeed a unity of God and man; God himself *creates* it; only God *can* create it; God creates it, because he wills to create it. It is no other unity than his own eternal unity as Father and Son. This unity is the Holy Spirit. He and he alone makes the unity of God and man necessary and possible. The Holy Spirit is God himself in his *freedom* to make his creature fit for communion with him, capable of receiv-

ing him, object of his revelation."[1] In other words the one
who is the unity of the triune God is the unity of God and
humanity in Jesus Christ and the same Spirit makes us able
to receive the Word incarnate as God's Word and work for
us.

In this act we see also the revelation of the free
grace of God corresponding to the divine election and manifesting it. Revelation is the revelation of the *truth* of God.
God is free in showing compassion, gracious because this
comes to us in spite of everything. For that reason it is at
the same time and must be reconciliation since it meets us
in our sin and makes us new creatures. In fact the mystery
of the incarnation is precisely this truth that a new creation
in the human Jesus takes place by the Holy Spirit. It is God
who is active here in new creative power.

Again, since in the incarnation the Word of God is
spoken to us and present with us, Barth underlines the fact
that Word and Spirit are never separated from one another.
Further, since the Holy Spirit is the union of God and humanity, it is the Spirit who manifests also the distinction
between God and humanity, Creator and creature. God is
God and not human and humanity is creature and can never become divine. The incarnation is not the divinising of a
creature nor is it saying that humanity in its fullest capacity
or filled with the Spirit is divine.

Barth points out in a way that has scarcely been
mentioned in any writings on the subject that the traditional
manner of relating God and humanity in the incarnation *anhypostasia* and *enhypostasia* is real by the Holy Spirit.
Pneumatology plays a key role in christological doctrine.
"The man Jesus as such has no existence of his own, no abstract existence that could be regarded separately, that
could have a separate meaning."[2] This is the negative side
of the two—the *anhypostasia*. The positive is that the human Jesus is given a true and real existence by the Word or
Son but this never takes place without the Holy Spirit. He is
enhypostatic in the Logos. "The man Jesus has his existence—*conceptus de Spiritu sancto*—directly and exclu-

sively in the existence of the eternal Son of God."[3]

Another way of stating the same truth is that humanity has no capacity for revelation, no inherent ability to receive the Word of God. Any capacity is a graced one. "The very possibility of human nature's being adopted into unity with the Son is the Holy Ghost. Here, then, at this fontal point in revelation, the Word of God is not without the Spirit of God. And here already there is the togetherness of Spirit and Word. Through the Spirit it becomes really possible for the creature, for man, to be there and to be free for God. Through the Spirit, flesh, human nature, is assumed into unity with the Son of God. Through the Spirit this man can be God's Son and at the same time the second Adam and as such 'the firstborn among many brethren' (Romans 8:29), the prototype of all who are set free for his sake and through faith in him."[4] Thus the negative, our incapacity and utter inability to be one with God because of sinful human nature, means that the Holy Spirit is the positive power uniting God and humanity; it is nothing in us that does so. Moreover the human Jesus has a representative role as the one for all and so becomes as firstborn son, the prototype of all believers who through the same Spirit also become sons of God. This view counters that of Roman Catholic dogmatics where there is a measure of reciprocity between God and humanity.

In line with traditional orthodoxy Barth affirms several things about the incarnation. At this particular point he follows the traditional formulae of orthodox christology but later on, while re-affirming these statements, he puts them in the different form of his doctrine of reconciliation. Here he affirms five things:

a) The incarnation is based on God's eternal will, choice and election to become the God of humanity. As such it is not simply incidental to the Fall, though it does deal with and overcomes human sin. God did not decide to become incarnate as a kind of afterthought when we had sinned, but his prior decision, action and will envisaged the Fall and the power to deal with it. In deciding in his eternal will to become incarnate he chose humanity for himself, chose to be our God and us to be his fellow partners.

b) The incarnation is intimately related to the life of the triune God. It is the Son and not the Father or the Holy Spirit who becomes incarnate; nevertheless, as Barth points out,[5] he does so in unity with the Father and the Holy Spirit. As the older theologians put it, the whole Trinity is involved in the incarnation. The external works of the Trinity are indivisible.

c) This only goes part of the necessary way. The Son became incarnate without any change, without ceasing in the slightest to be divine: "The statement that it is the Word or the Son of God who became man therefore asserts without reserve that in spite of his distinction as Son from the Father and the Holy Spirit, God in his entire divinity became man."[6] There is no giving away of any attributes as the theory of *kenosis* tried to say in the nineteenth century. There is no diminution of his deity whatsoever, however concealed or veiled he is in the flesh. One of the aspects of Barth's teaching is that this revelation of God in Jesus Christ is at the same time his concealment or his veiling.

d) The Son of God became incarnate, assumed our human nature into union with the divine and in so doing sanctified and made it whole and perfect. According to Barth, it was "flesh", sinful human nature that he assumed and this is to some extent contrary to the tradition. In the nineteenth century Menken and others in Germany and Edward Irving in England advanced the view that it was human nature in opposition to God that Jesus assumed but sanctified by his dwelling in it.[7] Again, there was no existing human being to whom the Son joined himself but the human Jesus came into being with the incarnation.[8]

e) The incarnation points to an incomparable union,[9] a personal union between God and humanity. With the Reformed tradition Barth underlines the union first but then goes on, perhaps more in the Lutheran tradition, to emphasize the two natures in the light of it. He envisages this union and communion in dynamic terms—the two natures of God and humanity in Jesus Christ enter, not only into a union, but into a fellowship and communion with one another. This act and these relationships are a given reality of revelation, a mystery. They can and must be affirmed as the central truth of the faith but cannot be either rationally deduced or explained. The *how* of God's act, its possibility remains a mystery.

B. THE VIRGIN BIRTH AND THE VIRGIN MARY

There is perhaps no point where the agreements and disagreements between Karl Barth and his Catholic critics are so clear as here in these doctrines. On the one hand he clearly affirms the traditional christology, the classical orthodoxy of the incarnation and the Virgin Birth—both in accord with Catholic teaching—and yet on the other hand he would not and does not acquiesce in the Catholic claims made for the Virgin Mary. It is here we can see where the points of divergence and agreement occur. Barth states the relationship between all three in this way; the incarnation is a mystery, indeed the *mystery* of God's action toward us in Jesus Christ. The Virgin Birth on the other hand is the *miracle* of grace by which this is effectuated and is its sign and the Virgin Mary is the agent of God's coming to us. Virgin Birth and Virgin Mary are thus related to the incarnation in this way; the Virgin Birth as the method of Jesus' coming, and the Virgin Mary as the agent. This is how Barth puts it, "In one way or the other the object to which they point is the event of the *incarnation*. But that general, inner, material thing of which they speak is the *mystery* itself and as such—that Jesus Christ is true God and true man. And the special, the outer thing, the sign of which they speak is the *miracle*—that Jesus Christ as this true God and man has *God* alone for his Father and therefore the *Virgin* Mary for his mother. The first is the fact of the free grace of God in his revelation. The second is the form and fashion peculiar to his revelation, in which as free grace it gives itself to be known."[10]

The Virgin Birth.[11]

If the incarnation is the reality of God's mysterious action in Jesus Christ his Son becoming incarnate and revealing God's true nature in our humanity, the Virgin Birth is the miracle which attests it. If the incarnation is the material content of the mystery the Virgin Birth is its form and sign, though having itself a true content. It points to the thing signified and is a parallel to the empty tomb at the resurrection. The Virgin Birth is, according to Barth, a sign and not the thing in itself; it simply indicates it. The sign therefore corresponds to and reflects the thing signified in such a way that if we are wrong in the one, we are likely to be wrong in the other, or, in other words, if one denies the Virgin Birth one may not have right views about the incarnation. It has, of course, been pointed out against Barth at this particular point that certain of the heretics in the Early Church believed in the Virgin Birth but did not affirm the incarnation. It is also true today that some theologians, like Emil Brunner,[12] affirm the incarnation, but do not accept the Virgin Birth. Nevertheless since the two are so closely associated, to deny the Virgin Birth may indicate that one has doubtful views about the incarnation as well. This at any rate is the view that Barth espouses.

Barth looks at this whole question from two perspectives—first of all the teaching of Holy Scripture and, secondly, the affirmations made in the dogma of the Creeds and Confessions attesting Scripture.

The New Testament[13] does not attest the Virgin Birth frequently but rather sparsely. The evidence is seemingly contradictory and not wholly conclusive. There are certain difficulties in the evidence—for example, the fact that it is only mentioned twice—in Matthew and Luke, that Joseph is mentioned as the father of Jesus, the fact also that it may be an insertion. All these point to difficulties. Nevertheless the stories are there and there is no adequate reason to doubt their authenticity. Rather they are to be affirmed and lead us to the dogma. Negatively, Barth states that the evidence does not lead us to deny the dogma. Joseph is simply the putative or legal father of Jesus and not the actual father, nor is the argument from silence—namely, that parts of the New Testament do not mention it indicative of the fact that the writers did not believe it. The question that is decisive here as elsewhere in coming to a final decision for or against is this: is it congruous with revelation as a whole? Is this the explanation that most suitably coheres with the totality of God's action in Jesus Christ, with the nature of Jesus Christ himself as divine and human? Does it point to this and indicate it more clearly than any other view? Barth has no doubt that the answer in this case is to affirm the Virgin Birth. As a miracle it points to the mystery of the incarnation of the Son of God. It points to God's sovereignty and majestic freedom in action for our salvation. It indicates on the one hand that here God is active as the subject and yet at the same time humanity is present in the person of the Virgin Mary. The Virgin Birth points to the *vere deus, vere homo*, true God and true man of the incarnation.

It is not, therefore, for Barth a matter of Christian liberty,[14] as some would suggest, whether we accept this or not. To reject it is to go against the truth it indicates and therefore may suggest a different, indeed a false christology. The argument of Brunner and others makes no impression on Barth. The heretics are the exceptions rather than the rule. The sign and the thing signified go together. The miracle points to the exceptional, unique person who is indicated in this way; so Barth affirms and so does Catholic teaching.

Barth next examines the credal statements *natus ex Maria Virgine*, (Born of the Virgin Mary) *Conceptus de Spiritu Sancto*. (conceived by the Holy Spirit).

Ex Maria.[15] This points to the real humanity of Jesus—the human son of an earthly mother. He was not born by male generation but by female conception. Yet, at the same time, it points truly to his humanity and also to the fact that humanity is there in the person of Mary. Humanity has a real place and presence in the event of the incarnation. Mary was really there, not in the sense of cooperating with grace, as in Catholicism, but as being the object and agent of the divine action. Barth writes, "He (real man) participates in it as a real man can, where God himself, God alone is the Subject, Lord and Master."[16] This is not to be understood in the sense of natural theology, where man has an innate capacity for God, but simply as man being there and being used by God in this way.

Ex Virgine.[17] This points to a miracle of the *grace* of God and not to any human action or possibility. It is God alone who is here active by the Holy Spirit. Further, it indicates the judgment upon humanity that is, that it has no power in itself to receive revelation. It is excluded from cooperation in the divine reconciliation. It is all of God and his grace and judgment. One can see clearly and already here that an affirmation of the same reality and truth—the Virgin Birth—leads to different ways of interpretation. For Barth it indicates the fact that it is all of God, of his grace and judgment and of the power of the Holy Spirit. For Catholicism it indicates humanity consenting to, agreeing with, co-operating with God in his action in the words of Mary assenting to the action of God in and through her.

But why a virgin? Barth speaks of the relative appropriateness of the female and the inappropriateness of the male. In his earlier writing on this subject he had made this the main reason for supporting the Virgin Birth, but in his later writing he makes this reason secondary. The male, he says, is inappropriate since Jesus is the eternal Son of the heavenly Father and not the Son of an earthly father, and therefore the male is excluded because God alone is the Father of the Son. And secondly, he is excluded since he is the dominant partner, the active rebel, the "lord" of woman. The female is appropriate since she merely receives and does not contribute; she is the chosen instrument of God and is made ready to receive Christ. This is not an entirely convincing argument, since the woman is not necessarily wholly receptive and also is a participant with man in the rebellion against God. But, for Barth, it is neither Mary's virginity as such nor her femininity that provides a point of contact. He does not believe in this point of contact since humanity is dead in trespasses and sins and cannot receive the divine of its own power. Rather it is God's grace shown in the choice of this humble vessel. The sign is not the absence of sin or the presence of an immaculate conception, but the absence of sinful, sexual life, the absence of humanity and the action of God the Holy Spirit. For Barth the judgment is on both male and female for their sin.

Conceptus de Spiritu sancto.[18] This points us to the real content and source of the miracle in God himself, to the centrality, importance and action of the Holy Spirit. For the Holy Spirit indicates God's sovereign freedom and grace and excludes all speculation from physics or biology. That physics or biology are involved in the Virgin Birth is not to be denied but this is not the central significance and meaning of it, because the Virgin Birth is not a natural, physical, human possibility, but a divine action.

The mention of the Holy Spirit has a double significance, first for Jesus Christ in his humanity and then for us.

For Christ it indicates that the mystery of God himself is manifest in the mystery of the humanity of Jesus Christ. It is God as Spirit who acts on his own behalf, creating among his creatures the possibility, power and capacity otherwise impossible. This power he gives to our humanity uniting it with the Word in Jesus Christ.

Secondly, on this basis and parallel to it, we, by the sheer grace of God in Jesus Christ, are prepared by the Spirit by God for God himself and so believe. There is thus an analogy in our being reconciled to the actual being and work of the Reconciler. The agent in each case is the Holy Spirit. Barth sums up these two emphases in these words: "The specific mention of the Holy Spirit as a more precise determination of the sign of the Virgin Birth is obviously significant in a twofold sense. In the first place, it refers back the mystery of the human existence of Jesus Christ to the mystery of God himself, as it is disclosed in revelation —the mystery that God himself as the Spirit acts among his creatures as his own Mediator, that God himself creates a possibility, a power, a capacity, and assigns it to man, where otherwise there would be sheer impossibility. And the mention of the Holy Ghost is significant here in the second place, because it points back to the connexion which exists between our reconciliation and the existence of the Reconciler, to the primary realization of the work of the Holy Spirit. For it is on this ground that the same work, the same preparation of man for God by God himself, can happen to us also, in the form of pure grace, the grace manifested in Jesus Christ, which meets us and is bestowed upon us in him."[19]

What Barth is saying here is this. Just as we receive Christ's grace by the Holy Spirit and as the Spirit fits and prepares us for it, so he fits and prepares our human nature in the person of the Virgin Mary to be the bearer of the Son of God. It is most suitable and appropriate therefore that the Holy Spirit who is the union of the divine life, who is the union of God and humanity in Jesus Christ, who is the agent of our reconciliation should be the agent of the divine coming into our life. Barth writes, "Through the Spirit it becomes really possible for the creature, for man, to be there and to be free for God. Through the Spirit flesh, human nature, is assumed into unity with the Son of God."[20]

Conceived by the Holy Spirit in no way means that Jesus is the Son of the Holy Spirit according to the flesh. He was not begotten by the Spirit; there was no marriage (*hieros gamos*) between the Holy Spirit and the Virgin Mary. It means rather that he (the Holy Spirit) is the agent of Jesus' birth. The Holy Spirit is God himself in his spiritual, miraculous act and not in a psycho-physical act.[21]

Again, consonant with Barth's views on revelation and the triune God, he follows the Protestant Lutheran post-Reformation theologian, Gerhard, and sees the whole Trinity involved:[22] we have God the Father in his creative omnipotence giving Mary power for this, God the Son making sinful human nature holy and his temple, God the Spirit the union of Father and Son uniting divine and human natures in one person.

One could summarize this as follows. The Virgin Birth as a sign points to the unity of God and humanity in Jesus Christ and is analogous to the mystery of God, Father, Son and Holy Spirit, who are one in the union of the same Spirit. The Holy Spirit is thus both the unity of the triune God, the agent of the incarnation, of the Virgin Birth and of our salvation. The conception by the Holy Spirit indicates a threefold perspective: an ontological, in its basis in the triune God; an incarnational, pointing to the ontic fact that it is God active here, God coming yet humanity graced and exalted, made fit for union with the divine; a soteriological, since it is indicative both of our total incapacity and of God's power to be free in his grace to bring us into union and fellowship with himself by the Word and Spirit.

NOTES

1. Karl Barth, *Credo*, trs. J. Strathern McNab, London: Hodder & Stoughton, 1936, p. 70. Barth's view would be very much opposed to the more radical writings on the Incarnation as seen in *The Myth of God Incarnate*, ed. John Hick, London: S.C.M. 1977. Brian Hebblethwaite, *The Incarnation, Collected Essays on Christology*, 1987 offers a more positive, orthodox approach and a measured critique of "The Myth".

2. Ibid., p. 60.

3. Ibid.

4. *C.D.*, I/2, p. 199.

5. Ibid., p. 33.

6. Ibid.

7. Ibid., pp. 151ff.

8. This teaching, as we have seen, is known as *anhypostasia* i.e., no human person existed as Jesus prior to the incarnation—no *hypostasis*. Rather *in* the Word he became *a* human person *enhypos tasia*.

9. *C.D.*, I/2, pp. 161ff.

10. Barth, *Credo*, pp. 62-63.

11. For this section see *C.D.*, 1/2, pp. 172-202 entitled "The Miracle of Christmas."

12. E. Brunner, *The Mediator*, trs. Olive Wyon, London: Lutterworth Press, 1934, pp. 322ff.

13. *C.D.*, 1/2, pp. 175-176.

14,. Ibid., p. 181.

15. Ibid., p. 185f . Barth takes only a christological interest in Mary; he rejects Roman Catholic teaching on Mary "*a limine.*" He believes it is a false growth adding both to Scripture and early Church teaching and must be excised. Moreover, it represents the supreme heresy of humanity co-operating by means of grace in its own salvation and thus threatens the sole Lordship of Jesus Christ. Barth' s answer to mariology is given in his christology where the human Jesus in union with the Son by the Holy Spirit is the basis and guarantee of our redemption. Volume IV/2 of the *Church Dogmatics* is a quiet, sustained dialogue with, and answer to, mariology. Barth writes: "The fact that the man Jesus is the whole basis and power and guarantee of our exaltation means that there can be no place for any other in this function, not even for the mother of Jesus." *C.D.*, IV/2, pp. ix-x. In his book *Ad Limina Apostolorum*, trs. Keith R. Crim, Edinburgh: The Saint Andrew Press, 1969, Barth recounts his experiences in Rome post Vatican II. In reply to a letter on Mariology by a Roman Catholic writer Barth states that he rejects the "possibility, justification and necessity of Mariology." (Ibid., p. 60).

16. Ibid., p. 186.

17. Ibid., pp. 187ff.

18. Ihid., pp. 196ff.

19. Ibid., pp. 199-200

20. Ibid., p. 199.

21. Ibid., pp. 200-201. see also *Credo*, p. 70. *Dogmatics in Outline*, trs. G. T. Thomson, London: SCM, 1949, p. 99.

22. Ibid., p. 201.

CHAPTER FOUR

HOLY SPIRIT AND HOLY SCRIPTURE

A. REVELATION AND SCRIPTURE

Traditional Protestant dogmatics generally began either with arguments about natural and revealed religion or with the doctrine of Holy Scripture. This was in line with the Reformation emphasis on the sole authority of the Scriptures as the only infallible rule of faith and practice. Karl Barth diverges from this in two ways,

a) He begins his *Dogmatics* with revelation and the Trinity and points out that he is following two of the few men in the past who took the same route, namely, Peter Lombard and Bonaventura in the Middle Ages.[1] He does so because he feels that anterior to our understanding of Holy Scripture and its nature must be our knowledge of God in his revelation. To be sure this revelation comes to us in and through Holy Scripture, but it is not Scripture itself that is our authority, but God speaking in and through it. Barth, therefore, can summarize his position by saying that while the Bible gives us the answer about revelation in this way "it has attested to us the Lordship of the triune God in the incarnate Word by the Holy Spirit."[2] He adds immediately,"but in so doing it has answered that question concerning itself which we have not yet asked."[3] Strictly for Barth revelation is God's coming, acting and speaking as the triune Lord, making himself known in Jesus Christ as the fulfilment of Israel's history by the power of the Holy Spirit.

b) Barth indicates his desire to remain true to Reformation insights about Holy Scripture, but departs at important points from their tendency towards a too literalist approach. For it is only in the light of revelation that we can understand what Scripture is, though, on the other hand, revelation comes to us through Scripture. The two, of course, belong together. Hence, in his *Church Dogmatics*, his treatment of Scripture comes chiefly within and in fact towards the end of his treatment of revelation. J. K. S. Reid exaggerates slightly, but his view of Barth's position is basically correct when he writes: "this represents a notable departure from the tendency especially evident in Calvinism to set the doctrine of Holy Scripture prominently in the forefront. Barth's presentation makes it clear from the start that a clean break has been made with the tendency in Protestant Orthodoxy to identify revelation with Holy Scripture."[4]

It is therefore obvious that for Barth Scripture does not stand alone, however much one emphasises the Reformation *sola scriptura*, by Scripture alone. It is related to the life of the Church first, through preaching based on it, and, secondly, as pointing us to the meaning and significance of it, namely, the place where God speaks his Word to humanity, the place of revelation. If in these various ways God speaks his Word to us, Barth can, in his early writings, speak of three forms of the Word of God—preached, written and revealed.[5] The order does not indicate an order of importance, but more of experience, though of course it must be said that the last is the primary form of the Word of God. Following Luther (and perhaps reflecting his own pastoral experience in preaching) proclamation comes first. This is grounded in and expounds Holy Scripture, and this again has as its meaning and basis God's act of revelation in Israel and in Jesus Christ. By this way of speaking Barth means to say to us: here are three inter-related and interdependent ways by which the triune God, revealed in the incarnate Lord, speaks to us by the Holy Spirit. In his later writings he modifies this way of speaking and uses the term "Word of God" primarily, indeed almost exclusively, for

God's self-revelation in Jesus Christ. Holy Scripture and preaching both bear witness to this, each in its own different way—Holy Scripture by being the permanent and inspired record of revelation and preaching based on this. Barth's interpreters dispute at this particular point whether this is a correction or a modification of his basic position and earlier emphases. The latter would seem to be the more correct and can be expressed in this way: "Barth's answer is clear. There is only one Word of God and definitive testimony is given to it by the apostles and prophets in the Old and New Testaments. Since, therefore, Jesus Christ declares himself through this testimony in a way that has binding authority for his community, preaching is bound to this and must, by the Holy Spirit, express it. One can therefore speak either of three forms of the one Word or of the one Word attested in Bible and Church. The Bible and Church stand together, the latter building on the former, and both coinciding and agreeing in an intimate way with the Word spoken in Jesus Christ. The former is, however, the definitive witness by which the Church exists."[7] Thus since Barth increasingly uses the word "witness" as he continues his writings in the *Church Dogmatics,* we can say that the Scriptures are the primary authority, the witness to revelation; the Church's proclamation becomes this in a derivative sense from the Holy Scriptures by the Holy Spirit. Perhaps the danger of the former way of speaking was that it could be misunderstood in the sense of a too immediate, almost direct identity between revelation, Scripture and preaching. For Barth the reality and possibility of such revelation rests only in God as he speaks and uses these means by the Holy Spirit. Walter Kreck,[8] a Reformed theologian strongly influenced by Barth, states that shortly before his death Barth spoke to a small group and indicated that he would no longer speak of the three forms of the Word of God. He used for preaching the illustration of the server at the Mass, who rings the bell which indicates the change that is said to happen but does not perform it; so preaching indicates the change that takes place when God comes and

speaks his Word through Scripture and proclamation. But it
is not the preacher who actually performs and brings the
Word of God. He is the medium of revelation.

B. THE NATURE OF SCRIPTURE

We have already indicated that Scripture is not the
thing signified but points to it and by the Word and Spirit
conveys it. This is sacramental language and Barth sees the
relationship between revelation and Scripture in this instrumental or sacramental light. Scripture is thus to be defined
as the primary, definitive, authoritative witness to divine
revelation. At this point it is necessary to say what Barth
means by witness, for it is not simply a human word with
merely human authority. It is indeed a human word, that of
the prophets and apostles of the Old and New Testaments,
but it is a word which stands in a unique relationship to the
object of testimony. G. W. Bromiley explains the particular
and very specialised way in which Barth uses this word
when he writes, "the word 'witness' is a dangerous one if
used in its ordinary sense, but if we think of the Bible as a
witness in the way in which the Bible itself describes the
prophets and apostles as witnesses —'he that receiveth you,
receiveth me'—it is perhaps not quite so objectionable as
some critics of Barth suppose."[9] Indeed it can scarcely be
called objectionable at all, and is now widely accepted by
modern scholars as the best way to describe Holy Scripture.
    The Scriptures are to be distinguished from revela-
tion as a human word, but at the same time to be regarded
as identical with it since revelation is its basis and object.
There is this two-foldness about it and there is therefore an
indirect identity between Bible and revelation or the Word
of God: "We distinguish the Bible as such from revelation"
as a witness to it. But since revelation takes place through
this testimony "the Bible is not distinguished from revelation."[10] Barth's favourite way of putting this is to say that
the Scriptures *become* and so *are* the Word of God as God
by his Spirit takes and uses them to speak ever and again to

humanity. And since Jesus Christ is the content of revelation he is the key, center and meaning of the Scriptures. They bear witness to him.

We look therefore at these two points briefly in turn to see their significance, First, the event character of the Scriptures, and Second, their relationship to Jesus Christ.

a) The Scriptures as an event.[11]

The Scriptures become and so are the Word of God. We can therefore say the Bible is the Word of God, but only in this sense. It indicates a special type of testimony which God takes and uses to come and to speak to us. Their authority is not simply in their words but in and through human words. They are not *per se* revelation but are instrumental thereto. The point that Barth makes here, as he does again and again, is that our hearing and receiving the Word of God does not come by our own doing, not even by our reading of the Scriptures, but is the miracle and mystery of God's grace, of his sovereignty. Our hearing and receiving are thus at his disposing. We cannot control revelation; God does. Now this does not mean that we do not use the Scriptures but simply sit back and wait. Quite the opposite. In fact, since Barth urges a listening to, a wrestling with the Scriptures to hear what God the Lord will say to us, we must use them diligently ever and again.[12] For here God who spoke in the past promises to speak in the present and we await his speaking now. Scripture has therefore a unique superiority for us and the Church as the place of God's promise, his presence in act, his speaking to us, the happening of his Word. Barth writes, "It is round this event that the whole doctrine of Holy Scripture circles, and with it all Church dogmatics, and with it, too, preaching and the sacrament of Church proclamation."[13] J. K. S. Reid interprets Barth thus, "Round this matter of event, the whole problem of Holy Scripture turns, as does also that of dogmatics, preaching, sacraments and proclamation. In the reality and truth of this event, there is nothing already past or only future, nothing that is pure recollection or pure expectation. In this event, this original witness is the Word of

God."[14] What this means is that as we have experienced, through the testimony of Scripture, God's revelation in the past and expect it in the future so these two, as it were, come together in God's act and speaking and we hear it as the Word of God now. Barth is saying clearly here that only God can speak his Word and he does it ever and again through the Holy Scriptures by the Holy Spirit.

   b) The Relation of the Scriptures to Jesus Christ.

   Since Jesus Christ is for Barth the center of faith and knowledge, and since the Scriptures testify to him, who he is will determine what the Scriptures are. Just as he is God and humanity in one, so the Scriptures have a divine-human aspect. The error of the older theology was to make the words too literally the Word of God, though they did not forget or omit the work of God's Spirit in illumining the pages of the Bible. Yet the parallel, as Barth readily acknowledges,[15] is only an imperfect one, for the words become the Word ever and again, whereas the union of God and man is permanent in Jesus Christ. There are two points of difference: (1) there is no unity of person between God and the humanity of prophets and apostles; (2) the humanity of prophets and apostles is not taken up into the glory of God as is the case with that of Jesus Christ. Nevertheless, Barth can say of the Bible, "It too can and must—not as though it were Jesus Christ, but in the same serious sense as Jesus Christ—be called the Word of God: the Word of God in the sign of the word of man, if we are going to put it accurately."[16]

   The form in which Barth sees the biblical witness to revelation is primarily, though not exclusively, narrative. The Word comes to us in story form similar to realistic novels.[17] The perspective from which the Gospel writers view the story of Jesus is that of the crucified One risen from the dead. Not only so but this is the key to the meaning of the whole biblical testimony. Barth gives impressive expositions of this in different parts of the *Church Dogmatics* and shows that he can combine both historical and other investigation of the text and a realistic theological interpretation of it. The historical factuality of the story of Jesus is important but it has special features, namely, those determined by the power and verdict of the Holy Spirit. It is, further, a story which by the same Spirit can be and is present to us today in renewing power.

C. THE INSPIRATION OF HOLY SCRIPTURE

In what has been said so far a particular view of God's relationship to and use of the Scriptures by the Holy Spirit is implied. Barth does not deny but affirms divine inspiration but seeks to give it a broader basis and interpretation than it received in traditional Protestantism. He argues that this was in fact the intention of the Reformers[18] even if it was not always actually carried out nor indeed could be fully carried out at the time of the Reformation. He agrees that the primary author of Scripture is God the Holy Spirit, whereas the writers are secondary authors, *secundarii auctores*, yet real human authors. How then are the two related? Barth sees Scripture, Holy Spirit and human response and receiving the Word as three aspects of the one work of God by the Holy Spirit and it is this in its totality that is *theopneustia* (divine inspiration).

Barth believes that there are three stages in the total process of inspiration,[19] (a) the fact of the revelation of God to Israel and in Jesus Christ; the hidden wisdom of God is there manifest; (b) the authoritative interpretation and speaking of it by the Holy Spirit; we have the mind of Christ, the thought of Christ on God's revelation; this eventually was crystallised both through oral and written tradition and became Holy Scripture; (c) the act of the same Spirit taking the written word and enabling us to understand. Barth himself describes it thus: "With all other men the witness stands before the mystery of God and the benefit of his revelation. That this mystery is disclosed to him is the first thing, and that he can speak of it the second . . . But the mystery of God, now entrusted to the human witness, will still remain a mystery . . . if the same Spirit who has created the witness does not bear witness of its truth to men, to those who hear and read. This self-disclosure in its totality is *theopneustia*, the inspiration of the word of the prophets and apostles."[20]

The weakness of much traditional teaching (both Catholic and Protestant) was that it took one aspect, the second, namely, the inspiration of the words and made it primary and almost exclusive. The tendency was to make the truths of Scripture a truth we can easily grasp and not a miracle of free grace. Indeed, the main criticism of Barth from both sides is that the human element as the divine word from God is undervalued at the expense of an exclusive emphasis on the act of grace—the event character of his speaking to us in Holy Scripture. For Barth, however, to put an additional reason in place of the reason God has given questions and endangers God's own way of acting. He agrees with Luther more than Calvin in this respect and states, "As Luther insisted in innumerable passages the word of Scripture given by the Spirit can be recognised as God's Word only because of the work of the Spirit which has taken place in it takes place again and goes a step further, i.e., becomes an event for its hearers or readers. How else will God be recognised except by God himself?"[21] This well expresses and underlines the characteristic emphasis of Barth throughout the whole of his theology: "Only by God is God known."

This does not mean any minimizing of the importance of the actual words. Barth accepts verbal inspiration but rejects what he calls verbal inspiredness. In other words there is no inherent efficacy in the words themselves. He believes that it was precisely this mistake that post-Reformation Protestantism committed;[22] it destroyed the mystery and the Bible became a part of the natural knowledge of God. It sought a certainty that was tangible, of works and not of faith. The human rather than being exalted in this process is really minimized and scarcely visible. For God speaks and gives by his Spirit (according to this view) even matters that we would know by ordinary means and this was certainly not the intention of Holy Scripture. The end result was that no discrepancies or errors at all could be admitted and the Bible became a "paper Pope", as Barth says, and "unlike the living Pope in Rome it was wholly given up into the hands of its interpreters. It was no longer a free and spiritual force, but an instrument of human power."[23] As a counterblast to this kind of literalism, perhaps as hyperbole, or to show the untenable nature of this position (which one would regard today as Fundamentalism) Barth posits the thesis that, even if the witnesses were at fault in every word, the true word by grace would and could be spoken in their human, erring and fallible words.[24] This is not a position that one can really defend, since the witnesses must surely be reliable in their interpretation, else their testimony is not valid. The best reason one can think of for this line of argument is that Barth is arguing *ad hominem.* In other words he is saying: if you take the words of the Bible to be wholly infallible, this does not prove the truth of revelation—it is God speaking through it that does,—any more than the view that they are wholly fallible and errant disproves it. It is God who uses this testimony and he alone who speaks his Word. Nevertheless, because of the very nature of the relationship of the witnesses to the original revelation, one must say that it is a trustworthy and reliable witness, and so to speak in this way is questionable if not in fact erroneous.

What Barth is always concerned to counter is a merely historical reading of Scripture, which, while necessary and proper in its place, and while using all the means of literary, historical and other forms of criticism, is but a preliminary to a real theological exegesis, to a listening to and saying after him what God the Lord is saying to us in his Word.

The two criticisms that have most frequently been levelled at Barth in this respect are (a) that the authority of Scripture is weakened unless we can prove its infallibility and inerrancy. How can this be done if we admit, as Barth seems to do, the possibility of mistakes? (b) Is his judgment that the Word of God is known as such only by God and through God not both an argument in a circle and does it not lead to a too subjective judgment? Yet writers who embrace a conservative view are Barth's defenders here. Gregor G. Bolich answers[25] (a) by making a distinction between "ontological", that is, inherent authority and "functional", that is, the authority of God. He writes of the Bible in support of Barth's view, "*Ontologically*, it is not infallible—if ontology is all that is being considered. Again Barth's actualism resolves the matter: the Scripture is not an 'in-itself, for-itself' entity but exists in the act of God's revelation, for God and for man, as the Word of God to man in the words of man himself. Scripture proves itself *functionally* infallible only in the act of God's gracious opening of human eyes to see Christ—and, once opened, human eyes behold the glory of God in the earthen vessel of human words. Thus one understands the inspiration of Scripture."[26] (b) On the second count G. W. Bromiley writes, "In no sense does he (Barth) think of a constitution of Scripture as God's Word by subjective experience of it. He has little time for inerrancy, which he seems to regard as both irrelevant and even misleading. On the other hand, while thinking that the possibility of error must be accepted, he can see no absolute position from which to establish actual errors and he sets no store by the emphasizing of alleged mistakes or difficulties . . . in what he has to say about the authority and freedom of Scripture as God's Word, Barth leaves little room for complaint."[27] On the question of the circular argument Barth believes this was essentially the method of the Reformers who taught that it is God the Holy Spirit (subjective revelation) who makes known to humanity objective revelation (the incarnation of the Word) attested in Holy Scripture. Scripture is in this way self authenticating. 'Scripture is recognised as the Word of God by the fact that it *is* the Word of God.' This is what we are told by the doctrine of the witness of the Holy Spirit . . . When we say 'by the Holy Spirit' we mean, by God in the free and gracious act of his turning to us. When

we say 'by the Holy Spirit' we say that in the doctrine of
Holy Scripture we are content to give the glory to God and
not to ourselves."[28]

Further, if we ask, but why this book alone, why a
canon?—Barth answers[29] that it was not brought about by
us but was simply recognised by the Church. The Church is
not the author of the canon. The central fact that made the
Church accept these and not other books was that they so
impressed themselves upon the mind of the Church by the
Holy Spirit as divinely inspired that it was felt one couldn't
do otherwise than acknowledge their authority.To that extent they are self-authenticating.

Yet Barth acknowledges that the decision in favour
of the canon is at the same time a limited human judgment.
Should new material emerge it can therefore be subject to
correction though in fact virtually closed. He writes, "Its
confession in this matter as in everything else can have no
final character nor be intended as more than a provisional
conclusion. The specific limits of the canon have in fact, in
ancient and modern times, been a matter open in principle
to the possibility of better instruction in the future concerning the concrete extent of that canon which the Church
knows as the unique, normative form of the Word of God.
But by no means does it follow that the Church can therefore take account in practice of any other normative form of
God's Word."[30]

D. SCRIPTURE AND TRADITION

Barth is aware of the fact that there is a question of
importance here and that it is not simply enough to state
sola scriptura or speak of the divine authority of Scripture
without indicating how he sees the relationship between
Scripture and tradition. The Scriptures are indeed the supreme authority or rather God speaking through them, *Dei
loquentis persona,* the Person of God speaking, as Calvin
said. Hence one cannot set up beside them or over them any
equal or higher authority. Neither the Church in its life and

tradition nor human reason must equal or be judge of the
Word of God. God himself is his own witness and interpreter of it and our attitude must be one of obedience.[31] The
Church in its life and tradition is always challenged anew
by this higher court, this authority, and yet strengthened at
the same time by the promise of Christ's presence in and
with the biblical testimony. So the Church and its tradition
"does not claim direct and *absolute* and material authority"
either for some third court of appeal or for herself, and
Barth adds "but for Holy Scripture as the Word of God."[32]
But the Church under it as obedient to the Word does have
a *relative* authority in its life, witness and tradition.

The phrase which sums up Barth's own attitude towards tradition in the Church is this: "respectful freedom in
relation to tradition." The respect comes first in relation to
decisions and people in the Church. There are three areas
where this respect should be manifest:[33] (a) in the decision
about the Canon in which the Church points beyond itself
to the Word; (b) in respect of the Fathers of the Church,
particularly the Patristic witness and the Reformers. There
can be no question of going back on the Reformation; we
must go on to complete it. This respect arises because of
the relative authority of these Fathers and their work, for
they stated as clearly and biblically as possible the essence
of the apostolic faith. There is respect too for the communion of saints as a living reality today; these are not simply
dead voices but living ones in the Church of Jesus Christ
giving a testimony to which we must faithfully listen and
give heed as interpreters of the Word. (c) This tradition of
our forefathers has been enshrined in Creeds and Confessions in which is set forth what they believed the Scriptures
taught. They are a testimony for truth and against error and
serve as a bond of union between members of the Church.
In them our fathers sought to expound the Scriptures and to
testify to their authority.

Yet this respect for tradition and traditional statements is and must be combined with a freedom of the Word
and under the Word, a freedom to look at past statements

and formulate them anew. It may be that we will come to exactly the same conclusions as did our forefathers at Chalcedon, for example, in their christological statement. But the very nature of confession in the Reformed tradition makes the possibility of revision ever open. Barth writes, "If divine infallibility cannot be ascribed to any Church confession, then in practice we have to recognise that every Church confession can be regarded only as a stage on a road which as such can be relativised and succeeded by a further stage in the form of an altered confession. Therefore respect for its authority has necessarily to be conjoined with a basic readiness to envisage a possible alteration of this kind."[34]

So the ultimate authority is the Word of God spoken again and again in and to the Church on the basis of the biblical testimony. This in turn creates a tradition of faith, fellowship and confession all of which have a relative authority as they seek faithfully to reflect the true light of the Word.

NOTES

1. *C.D.*, 1/1, p. 300.
2. *C.D.*, 1/2, p. 457.
3. Ibid.
4. J.K.S. Reid, *The Authority of Scripture*, London: Methuen, 1957, p. 195. For a discussion of Barth's doctrine in the context of the *Church Dogmatics* see Christina Baxter, "The Nature and Place of Scripture in the Church Dogmatics", in *Theology Beyond Christendom*, 1986, pp. 88-135.
5. *C.D.*, 1/1, pp. 88-124.
6. *C.D.*, IV/3,1, pp. 113ff.
7. J. Thompson, *Christ in Perspective*, Edinburgh, The Saint Andrew Press, 1978, pp. 116-117.
8. Walter Kreck, in Berthold Klappert, *Promissio und Bund, Gesetz und Evangelium bei Luther und Barth*. Göttingen: Vandenhoeck und Ruprecht, 1976, pp. 272-273.

9. G. W. Bromiley, *Karl Barth's Doctrine of Inspiration*, quoted by Colin Brown, in *Karl Barth and the Christian Message*, London: Tyndale Press, 1967, p. 32.

10. *C.D.* 1/2, p. 463.

11. Ibid., p. 464f.

12. See Karl Barth, *God Here and Now*, trs. Paul M. van Buren, London: Routledge and Kegan Paul, 1964, pp. 51-55.

13. *C.D.*, 1/2, p. 503.

14. Reid, op.cit., p. 214.

15. *C.D.*, 1/2, p. 513.

16. Ibid., p. 500.

17. See David F. Ford, "Barth's Interpretation of the Bible", in *Karl Barth - Studies of his Theological Methods*, S. W. Sykes, ed. pp. 55-87; and David H. Kelsey, *The Use of Scripture in Recent Theology*, Philadelphia: Fortress Press, 1975, pp. 39ff.

18. *C.D.*, 1/2, pp. 519-522.

19. Ibid., p. 51 4ff., I Cor. 2:16. Otto Weber, *Foundaions of Dogmatics*, Vol. 1. trs. Darrell L Guder, Grand Rapids: Eerdmans, 1981, p. 237 is in substantial agreement with Barth in seeing theopneusty in the context of "the totality of the biblical witness." (ibid.).

20. Ibid., p. 516.

21. Ibid., p. 521.

22. Ibid., pp. 522ff.

23. Ibid., p. 525.

24. Ibid., pp. 529-530.

25. G. Bolich, *Karl Barth and Evangelicalism*, Illinois Inter-Varsity Press, 1980, pp. 147-148. Both Weber, op. cit., p. 272 and Donald Bloesch, "The Primacy of Scripture" in *The Authoritative Word. Essays on the Nature of the Scripture*, ed. Donald McKimm, Grand Rapids: Eerdmans, 1983, pp. 136ff. take a similar view of Barth.

26. Ibid.

27. G. H. Bromiley, *Introduction to the Theologv of Karl Barth*, Edinburgh: T. & T. Clark, 1979, pp. 43-44.

28. *C.D.*, 1/2, p. 537.

29. Ibid., pp. 473ff.

30. Barth, *God Here and Now*, pp. 49-50; cf. *C.D.*, 1/2, pp. 473ff.

31. *C.D.*, 1/2, pp. 538ff.

32. Ibid., p. 538; italics mine.

33. Ibid., pp. 597ff.
34. Ibid., pp. 658-659.

CHAPTER FIVE

THE HOLY SPIRIT, RECONCILIATION AND RESURRECTION

A. RECONCILIATION

In traditional Protestant dogmatics various divisions in Christian doctrine were recognised in relation to Jesus Christ. First there was the *person* of Jesus Christ as the God-man. Secondly, there was the *work* of Jesus Christ in atonement—generally taught under the three offices, as they were called, of prophet, priest and king. Thirdly, there were the two *states* of humiliation and exaltation, the humiliation representing Jesus coming into this world, living in it, enduring suffering and bearing our sins in his death on the cross. The exaltation consisted in rising from the dead, ascending to heaven and reigning with the Father.

This was all very clear and logical but has been queried in our day by Karl Barth.[1] While he applauds the clarity, system and logic of this arrangement he has certain questions to put to it and certain objections. He wants to and does affirm the orthodox doctrines of the Council of Chalcedon (451 A.D.) that Jesus is both God and man. He also accepts that Christ humbled himself to us and was exalted, that he bore our sins in his atoning life and death through his priestly office, and that he was also king and prophet. However, Barth looks at these three areas of person, work and states again and shows how, while they have this impressive clarity, at the same time the older dogmatics tended to separate these aspects of the Christian revelation that should not be isolated and divided. Jesus Christ is one and undivided in all his ways and works. Moreover, this method also isolated Christ from the Church and had at the same time, as its presupposition, a doctrine of sin. Barth, on the contrary, sees Christ in his unity and totality as always related to the Church, as alone truly showing up the nature of sin, and as bringing justification. He also indicates that the older doctrines—particularly in relation to the person of Christ—dealt with the incarnation at the beginning and the atonement at the end, the one related to the coming of Christ and the other related to the end of his life, but tended to neglect the center and left a gap there. Barth himself tried to fill this gap and he gives a very powerful exposition of Jesus Christ as he is seen in the Gospels as the royal man.[2] He believes that one should look at these questions again and see the reality of Christ as one; he does this in his massive doctrine of reconciliation.

We recall that for Barth a central concept is that of revelation. God is known to us in his revelation in Jesus Christ. But since humanity is in a sinful state before God, this revelation can only come as reconciliation, that is, through God not just manifesting himself in Christ, but acting on our behalf in atoning and saving power.

The doctrine of reconciliation, as Barth sets it out, is one of his greatest achievements and is a very powerful piece of concentrated exposition. How does he look at it? He sees Jesus Christ as one in the totality of his being and action. He takes the parable of the prodigal son as a kind of illustration and relates Christ to this.[3] He sees the divine-human person, the two states of humiliation and exaltation and the three offices of prophet, priest and king, as one in Jesus Christ.[4] Yet he too must, for the sake of truth and clarity, make certain distinctions and emphases. In the light of the parable of the prodigal son, Barth interprets Jesus Christ as the *Son of God* in obedience to the Father going into the far country of human disobedience, there *humbling* himself and at the same time accomplishing our salvation through *atonement,* through his *priestly* work. In other words he takes three of the old views of traditional dogmatics and sees them as one, viz., the divinity of Christ, his humiliation and his priestly office. But at the same time as this movement towards humanity takes place there is a movement upwards as well, the *exaltation* of humanity in Jesus Christ, the Homecoming of the *Son of Man.* By his union with the Son of God Jesus is seen as *true man,* royal man, humanity exalted to perfect fellowship with God, obedient man, or, as he sometimes calls him, "reconciled man", exercising *kingly* authority and rule. In other words here Jesus as human, the state of exaltation and the kingly rule or office of Christ are one—a second aspect or movement in the one divine action. Thus there is a movement downwards which produces a movement upwards but these are simply aspects or moments of the one action of God in Jesus Christ. Thirdly, there is a movement or direction outwards; the one *Lord Jesus Christ* having completed objectively the work of reconciliation in his life, death and resurrection, is now himself the true *witness* as the God-man. Jesus testifies as *prophet* to what he has done, and shines as light in the darkness of the world by the power of the Holy Spirit. In this third aspect of the doctrine of reconciliation Barth sees the *God-man*, the *unity* of Christ and the *prophetic office* of Christ as one. Christ is his own prophet declaring his reconciliation, showing it forth as light in the world and enabling men and women to believe by the power of the Holy Spirit.

Here then are the basic thoughts of this doctrine of reconciliation in which there is a great symmetry, an architectonic.[5] In the light of the first movement—God's coming down—human sin is seen as *pride*, the sin of exalting oneself. God overcomes this in *justification* and the *calling* of the *Church* and of the *individual* to *faith* within it.[6] In the second aspect of reconciliation—humanity's exaltation—sin is seen as *sloth*. Where God lifts us up and exalts us we drag ourselves down by disobedience and sin. But God by his grace and Spirit makes us holy, *sanctifies* us, *builds* us up in the *Church* of Jesus Christ and individually, personally in *love* within the Church.[7] In the third aspect, which in many ways is the most exciting, interesting and attractive of all, Barth sees sin as falsehood. Jesus Christ is the true witness, the witness to his own truth and humanity lives a lie by acting against truth. In this aspect it is made to know the truth. The Church is a missionary Church and Barth speaks in an extremely helpful way about the mission of the Church. It is to be a light in the world reflecting the light of Christ and human beings in the Church live in *hope*.[8]

     In all this Barth shows us the true, dynamic reality of Christ's being and action. He objects to the old idea of states because they do not show the being of God in his action. This means that since God is known in Jesus Christ we must see him as a whole in the totality of his being and action, which are one. Nevertheless within this unity and totality one must make proper distinctions and give a certain priority to christology which determines all the rest.

B. CROSS AND RESURRECTION

     If it is true that reconciliation has these aspects, as Barth affirms, there is nonetheless a center from which he starts out to view the whole. It can be put in this way. Jesus Christ is the Reconciler in the whole of his being and action. But if the center of God's action and its meaning is in Christ, in revelation and reconciliation, the center of Jesus Christ is to be seen in the cross and resurrection. In fact this is the place from which Barth's whole theology begins. It is essentially a theology of the cross viewed in the light of the resurrection. He sees the cross which is the supreme contradiction of God as the place where the true nature of God is revealed, God as he truly is. It is for this reason that Barth rejects natural theology, because no natural theology could ever see that the cross was the revelation of the very nature and heart of God. It is also for this reason that he rejects the gods of man's devising, the philosophical and other ideas which men have of God which he simply regards as idols, as false conceptions of God, nonentities. God has given us the true picture of himself in the atoning cross of Jesus Christ and there is no need for any other. Nor does it mean that one is unsympathetic towards the views of others or their culture, but that one cannot and must not in any way minimize the significance and centrality of the fact that in the cross is the revelation of the true God. For Barth everything has been done in the cross and the whole life of Jesus centers and focuses on and leads up to this point. Here we see the deity of Christ revealed.[10]

While Barth emphasises the unity of Christ he also treats the atonement in a separate section—the Judge judged in our place.[11] His view is that Jesus Christ coming into our sinful situation must come as Judge, the Lord who dethrones us from our attempt to usurp God's place, the One who in a strange reversal of roles becomes the one judged in our place. This he does in our history in space and time by his passion and death. As man he replaces the old Adam and brings to view the new creation. In this way God is both gracious and just, the righteous God and righteous humanity in one. It is also by our incorporation into Christ the Reconciler that we become and are Christian.

But the whole life of Christ including his death would be meaningless for us were it not for what followed. The resurrection is supremely important and central to Barth's whole *Church Dogmatics* as it is to Christian faith and life. Indeed he is prepared to go so far as to say that it is the period of the forty days which is the revelation of God because here men and women saw Jesus as he truly was. This does not mean that the rest of the life of Jesus, including his cross, is unimportant but rather that it is only from this perspective and in this light that one sees its meaning. Were it not for the resurrection the cross would, in a sense, be a dead letter. What happened there, what was accomplished there would be closed off from us. Thus in Barth's doctrine of reconciliation the resurrection takes a central place.[12]

The relevance of this can be seen in this way. Barth asks the question, How does what has happened in Jesus, his reconciling us to himself, and fulfilling the covenant God made with Israel come to be ours, since we are separated from it? In one sense, he says, we are included because Christ is representative man and all that has happened in the atonement includes us. On the other hand we are separate from it, both by time and by sin. The two answers which Barth gives as to how this comes to us are the resurrection and the Holy Spirit; here is the relationship between reconciliation, resurrection and the Holy Spirit. All that is necessary for the salvation of the whole world and of all humanity has been accomplished. We are all included in what Christ has done for us in his life and death. Not only so but here God reveals himself both as true God and the perfection of humanity in atonement. Now all this comes to us because it is opened up by the resurrection and brought home to us by the Holy Spirit.

It will therefore be necessary to look briefly at how Barth views the resurrection. He does so under five headings:[13]

a) First, Barth affirms the reality of Christ's resurrection as a divine act and he distinguishes between the awakening (*Auferweckung*) and resurrection (*Auferstehung*) though they naturally cannot be separated. The awakening is the act of God the Father in raising his Son Jesus from the dead, whereas the resurrection is his appearing alive to his disciples on the basis of his awakening. He writes, "It is one thing that he 'rises again' and shows himself to his disciples (resurrection) as the One raised again from the dead (John 21:14). Quite another thing is the act of this awakening."[14] Barth sees this as based on Holy Scripture. In the first Jesus is the object and recipient primarily, though one can to some extent speak also of Jesus himself rising from the dead. This, however, Barth sees as something that is primarily given to him by the Father, whereas in the second he is subject and active. In his doctrine of reconciliation one of the important points is that of the obedience of the Son to the Father. The Son does all in obedience to the Father and is subordinate to him; this is true of his eternal being as well as of his temporal existence. This in no way threatens or impugns his equality with the Father. Here it is primarily the Father who acts in the resurrection of Jesus Christ from the dead. In raising Jesus from the dead we have the true and distinctive character of revelation shown to us and so see the cross, life and work as manifesting the deity of Jesus Christ. It is in the resurrection that the same man Jesus appears to his own and is seen and known as such. The crucified Lord Jesus is now seen in the resurrection. In this way he is present both as Lord and God; Barth can therefore speak of the awakening of Jesus Christ from the dead as the exemplary form of revelation. He says it is "the revelation of God . . . the true, original, typical form of the revelation of God in him."[15]

Again, he can speak of it as a free act of divine grace of the Father to the Son. It is by the grace of the Father that the Son is raised from the dead, so that Barth can say, "no, not simply as man but even as the Son of God Jesus Christ is here simply the One who takes and receives, the recipient of a gift."[16] It is thus the exclusive action of the Father to and upon the Son who was obedient to him. When we relate this to his preceding life we can say that the resurrection revealed that "he had always been present among them in his deity though hitherto this deity had been veiled."[17] There was no time therefore when he was not truly, wholly and fully God; therefore his deity centered in his cross and its reconciliation and revealed in the resurrection is the truth of his life as a whole. The relationship between the resurrection and his preceding life is that hitherto what he really was was concealed but now it is fully manifest. Now he is revealed as the God he was. For Barth therefore the resurrection has this retrospective significance. This means that he is opposed to those who, like Pannenberg, give to this awakening or resurrection what he (Pannenberg) calls a retroactive significance, that is, it acts back and in some sense both confirms and also effects the unity of Jesus with God.

b) Barth speaks of the resurrection as a new, independent act of God. It is not simply the explanation of the meaning of the cross—its other, reverse side, as Bultmann says,[18] nor is it simply to be identified as the rise of faith in the first disciples, as Bultmann again indicates.[19] Rather it is a new act in relation to the cross, though obviously continuous with it.

For Barth it is God's confirmation of the cross, the verdict of approval of the Father on the obedience and atoning work of the Son. Had God not so acted and given his "yes" of approval, the cross would have remained a tragic riddle and death would have been *de facto* recognised as in control.

But in the resurrection this is denied and Christ is raised. The crucified One is manifest in bodily form to faith as the risen One. In the totality of his being he appears to his own and so exalts humanity to union and fellowship with himself. But faith must see and accept this and over this we have no disposal or power. Only the Holy Spirit creates such faith and enables us to penetrate and receive this mystery which is true revelation. Here there is a threefold cord, God justifies himself, his Son and us. He shows his own right ways, that of his Son and our righteousness in him.

c) There is a positive relationship between the cross and resurrection because it is the one Lord Jesus Christ who is present in both and what happens in each concerns us. There is, one could say, a positive and a negative side. The resurrection reveals the positive side of what happens negatively on the cross. It has at the same time the negative event of the cross as its necessary presupposition. There is thus a unity between them but in this irreversible order.

Again, the two are related as *contemporaneous*. The risen One is the crucified One and the resurrection brings before us the crucified Lord now. The gulf between then and now is overcome in Jesus rising and being the Lord of time. The resurrection thus does not deny this historicity or reality of the cross but makes it a present reality for us. But there is also a temporal sequence. Just as there is an interval between them and a different form of presence so his presence today is temporally and actually different from then. After the resurrection and today he is present in and as his community in the world.

d) The resurrection has a spatio-temporal, that is, a historical dimension. The appearances are real, they take place in our space and time. Yet Jesus is present in a different way from the pre-resurrection period where history can prove his actual reality. The resurrection, while a real event in space and time, cannot be proven by historical means. Yet it really happened; the disciples saw the Lord present in bodily form. The empty tomb is but a sign of the real event and its significance which is only apprehended by faith.

To deny the resurrection objective reality would be to deprive it and the cross of real meaning. This again is spoken against Bultmann who simply makes the resurrection an aspect of the cross.[20] Faith however is not the meaning and basis of the apostolic testimony to the risen Lord. Rather the risen Lord created faith in the disciples in conflict with their own unbelief. The way in which the disciples actually experienced the Lord cannot, according to Barth, be expressed but that he was present with them creating a real faith in them and in his living presence is undeniable.

e) The relationship between the cross and the resurrection is irreversible yet inseparable in the one Lord. Therefore both must be understood, spoken of and realized together. To have a theology of the cross alone is to be avoided, just as is all piety which looks simply at the cross. For Christ is risen; he is risen indeed. To concentrate solely on the cross would be to break the unity and end in mythology. The one crucified and risen Lord Jesus is, according to the Barmen Confession of 1934, the one Word of God.

It is therefore in this two-sided, irreversible unity that cross and resurrection are ours, as our death and new life, the death of our sin and the new life hidden with Christ in God.

C. THE HOLY SPIRIT

Now while all this has been done for us in our humanity as Christ died for our sins and rose for our justification, it is only objectively real. The question is, how does it become ours, how do we as humans participate in this subjectively? Barth's answer is that this takes place by the Holy Spirit.[21] It is the Spirit of the risen and exalted Lord Jesus who comes and makes real for us and in us what has happened in the whole Christ event. We are thus incorporated into him, so that when we speak of Jesus Christ we never think of him in isolation but always as "Jesus Christ and his own." In other words the power of the resurrection is realized as the power of the Holy Spirit now, creating faith and a community of God's people. The power of the resurrection reveals and applies the power of the atoning work of Christ.

The Holy Spirit of the crucified, risen, ascended Lord creates and sustains the community in the time between the ages, the first and second coming of Jesus Christ, giving freedom from slavery and disobedience, life and joy in the darkness of our existence, true knowledge corresponding to God's self knowledge and the peace of God's reconciliation in Christ, peace with others and with oneself. Finally, the Spirit gives life lived in harmony with God and in obedience to his will, but all this in no isolated existence but in the community of faith it creates. To put it in Barth's type of language we could say: just as humanity is exalted in Jesus Christ by virtue of his humiliation, so the Holy Spirit as God's power and presence lifts us up and exalts us in the totality of our being to participate in the divine life of God, Father, Son and Holy Spirit and to a life corresponding to his.[22]

Thus in the action of the Holy Spirit we meet and experience the power of the resurrection and this Barth can describe as Christ in the power of all he was and did stretching out his arm, as it were, and drawing us into the welcome embrace of his fellowship. In this way he is per-

sonally present and active[23] and does not give over his
Lordship either to ecclesiastical institutions (as in Catholicism) or pious individuals (as in Liberal Protestantism). He
does not need any "sacramentally or existentially endowed
vicars"[24]—as in Catholicism and Bultmann.

The Spirit is thus always the Spirit of the one Word
of God in the one whole Lord Jesus Christ and is never
simply the Spirit of inwardness or mysticism. In this way
all that Christ is and has done is ours in the Spirit and in
fellowship with his people. Barth can also point to the fact
that this is not simply a christological doctrine and basis,
but a trinitarian one. Just as God moves within himself as
the one who has life within himself, as Father and Son mu-
tually love one another in the power and fellowship of the
Holy Spirit, so by the same Spirit we are invited and enabled to participate in the very life of the triune God and to
reflect this in our existence. Again, Barth can say, the history that takes place between Jesus and us in the Spirit reflects, is analogous to, the history of love between Father
and Son in the Holy Spirit.[25]

But what specifically does it mean to receive and
have this life, to walk in the Spirit? Barth underlines three
ways in which this is seen in us.

a) The Holy Spirit gives *direction* pointing us to
true wisdom, the reality of our true being and freedom in
Jesus Christ. We are directed by the Spirit and enabled to
be what we are. Beside the indicative stands the imperative.

b) This direction at the same time includes a *correction* pointing out possibilities of true freedom and warning
against the ways of disobedience, unfreedom and death,
which are no true but false ways. For this reason the Spirit
also groans for us and prays for us, so that those who know
the reconciliation of God in Christ may not enter into any
pact with the world.

c) The Holy Spirit also *instructs* us, revealing to us
the ways and will of God with concreteness and authority—the ways that correspond to our being and freedom in
Jesus Christ.

The Holy Spirit as the Spirit of the reconciling and risen Christ points and guides us to what we are in Christ with a backward glance at his being and action and a forward one to the freedom to which we are called in fellowship with him.

Several points may be made in relation to this whole exposition.

In the first place there is the impressive way Barth has restructured traditional doctrine to make it conform more fully to the unity of the being and work of Jesus Christ. This is definitely a step forward and avoids the dangers of division between who Christ is and what he does. Being and work are one.

Secondly, the concentration and the focus on the cross and resurrection does not mean a discarding of the incarnation but an emphasis on the fulfillment of the life and history of Jesus in atoning sacrifice and victorious conflict. It is his life-history in the totality of his being and action that is the revelation of God and the reconciliation of humanity with God. Particularly important is the way in which the differentiated relationships of the cross and resurrection are interwoven and give us the key to the nature of the humiliated One who is also exalted and whose action shows us who Jesus is as divine and human.

Thirdly, Barth presents an inclusive christology, that is, one which not only emphasizes the reality of God's being and action in Christ but the fact of all humanity being included in this reconciliation. The universality of the atonement points to Christ as representative human being is an implicate of it and avoids the difficulties and pitfalls of a limited atonement particularly associated with scholastic Reformed doctrine. Jesus Christ is the one person who is for all humanity. Barth's views have their own problems— the danger of universalism and the relationship between a view ontologically (*realiter*) including all but noetically (*actualiter*) involving only a limited number. Barth does not seek to reconcile these two aspects logically, but answers our queries by pointing to the freedom and sovereignty of God by the Holy Spirit. He is the free Lord in his grace towards us, yet this freedom must imply a consistency of God with himself.

Fourthly, the resurrection is both a new creative act of God but also the revelation of his verdict on the cross. It answers the question of the participation of the whole human being in the person and work of Jesus Christ, the question of its significance for us. In showing the crucified *human* Jesus as the risen Lord of all Barth is pointing to the significance of the humanity of Christ for our Christian life and our eternal salvation. In other words without the bodily resurrection of the Crucified the reality of our human participation in Christ is jeopardised and the work of the Spirit would be quite different.

Fifthly, in moving from the area of God's action in Christ to our participation in salvation Barth maintains strongly that he is not departing from his christological basis but underlining it in a new way and with a new emphasis. Here Rosato's view that Barth's doctrine of reconciliation is primarily pneumatological cannot be fully supported. It has this thrust but must have an objective basis in reconciliation in Christ. By the Holy Spirit we do not leave Christ or christology behind for the Spirit is Christ's own spiritual being and work within us. The word of reconciliation in Christ is thus a word pregnant with spiritual power. This accords with the New Testament emphasis on the Lord as Spirit. Yet the Spirit is not Christ but distinct from him, God in another form, God present to his creatures. While, therefore, it is true that the Holy Spirit is the transition or mediation between Christ and Christians it is at the same time and always the Spirit of Christ and no separate Spirit acting independently. Christology and pneumatology are intimately interconnected.

Sixthly, with this whole conception of reconciliation Barth has broadened and enriched his christological center but not changed it. Earlier in the *Church Dogmatics* he began with the traditional view of the incarnation but here he begins from the perspective of the cross and resur-

rection. The reality of our salvation cannot be comprehend-
ed save as we follow to the end and rightly interpret the story of Jesus' life and ministry with its unbelievable climax in
the cross and beyond in the resurrection. Yet, paradoxically, this deepest humiliation is the highest height of God's
grace. It is this that the resurrection reveals and the Holy
Spirit conveys. It is here that we meet with God. As Klappert[27] reminds us in his interpretation, the cross is taken up
into our understanding of the very nature of the triune God
and his action toward us. Here is no monologue in heaven
or eternal history played out above our heads but the full
entry of God into our history, state and place to lift us up to
himself. It is a great misunderstanding of Barth to see the
Trinity and election as isolated from the life and work of
Christ and the Church or as dominating and overshadowing
the actual history of Jesus Christ. It is rather from the reality of this history of our reconciliation in the life, death and
resurrection of Christ that we know God as he is—the
triune God who in his eternal will purposed and acted for
our salvation.

Finally, in this section Barth is raising the acute
question of how the Jesus of yesterday, of "there and then"
becomes a reality and has effect in our life today. Is it simply a question of bringing the Jesus of yesterday into the
world of today? Is the relation between him and us by the
Spirit merely temporal and geographical so that an answer
would lie both in historical succession and tradition, human
mediation or in the outreach to all peoples? These are indeed involved and should not be minimized. The Spirit is
active in all these ways. But the real question is not the dis-
tance between God and us temporally but, one might say,
spiritually, between God the Holy Judge who is for us yet
against us because we are against him in our sin. It is this
chasm that must be bridged and not merely the temporal or
geographical one. That his holiness did not merely destroy
our sin but gave us a new humanity, a future beyond our
end as sinners is due to God's grace in Christ. The bridge
between God and us is made available by the power of the
Spirit whom J. V. Taylor calls the Go-Between God.[28] It is

in this way that the reconciliation of yesterday becomes our reconciliation with God today and we become and are members of Christ and the Church.

D. ON BEING A CHRISTIAN

Barth can put this in simple terms by saying that what we are dealing with here is how a person becomes a Christian—by the revelation of Christ's resurrection and in the power of the Holy Spirit. He writes, "This, then, is our answer to the question how it is possible and actual, and can be said in truth, that a man becomes and is a Christian."[29] It is not at all our work but the work of God; yet it is at the same time wholly our work since we believe. The miracle and paradox of grace and faith are here.

Now this view is in marked contrast to those of Rudolf Bultmann[30] and Roman Catholicism both of which Barth opposes at this point.

Bultmann sees the New Testament as set in a framework of mythological language requiring to be demythologised. Little can be known of the life-history of Jesus Christ and what we do know must be reinterpreted in the light of man's self-understanding. This is in fact what the New Testament itself demands and is the key to its proper interpretation. But this self-understanding is partially the same as that of existential philosophy as interpreted by Heidegger. Hence a philosophical self-understanding determines in part our interpretation of the New Testament.

The center of the New Testament message is the cross and resurrection. But the resurrection is not, as for Barth, a new act of God in raising his Son Jesus Christ from the dead. Rather it reveals the significance of the cross as saving event; it is its reverse or noetic side. But the cross and resurrection so understood are known by us through the kerygma—the proclamation we find in Scripture and in Christian preaching. In receiving it we die and rise with Christ, or, as Bultmann puts it, "make the cross of Christ our own,"[31] as God's action for us. Who Jesus Christ is is not a question of prime importance. What is important is the significance of the preached message for me as the eschatological event here and now. This is how a person becomes and is a Christian.

Barth rightly believes that, in putting the Christian faith in these terms, Bultmann is distorting the New Testament testimony to Jesus Christ. Bultmann and the preachers then become "existentially endowed vicars".[32] The pre-understanding of Existentialism partly at least determines our interpretation of Jesus Christ and the New Testament message about him. The demythologising is but the negative side of Bultmann's real programme which is to give us his particular version of the Christian faith; this at any rate is how Barth sees it.[33] The result is a clear indication of the inadequacy of the method and its presuppositions. It leaves us with a minimal christology—a Christ whose resurrection almost disappears, a Christ-event which largely merges with the kerygma and a kerygma which is only real as God acts through it and we by our human decision die and rise to new life. This is what is meant by making the cross of Christ our own, by becoming a Christian. But can the cross of Christ and the resurrection be properly interpreted when reduced to their significance for me? Does this not both seriously reduce the content of the Christian revelation and make it individualistic with an eschatology which is a *nunc aeternum*—eternity here and now? In other words the significant, objective reality of God's reconciling act in Jesus Christ as the object of our faith and the basis and content of the kerygma are only real in faith's decision and their significance for me. This is the consequence of seeking to put the revelation of God in Christ in the cross and resurrection within the framework of an existentialist metaphysic.

But, says Barth, "Jesus Christ cannot be absorbed or dissolved in practice into the Christian kerygma, Christian faith and the Christian community."[34] As the crucified and risen One who has reconciled us to himself and revealed this in power he is not dependent on nor predetermined by our presuppositions. He may certainly use and does use representatives, but, in so doing, he is not predetermined by them. He remains and acts as the sovereign Lord coming by the Holy Spirit in the fullness and power of an objective, completed reconciliation. The One who came and is to come needs no existential representatives who predetermine his action and limits, but is the free Lord of the present as of the past and future. To speak of the Christian faith as Bultmann does strikes both at the content of the faith and at the Lordship and freedom of the crucified and risen Christ to act by the Spirit directly upon us.[35]

NOTES

1. *C.D.*, IV/l, p. 123f.
2. *C D.*, IV/2, pp. 154-264.
3. Ibid., pp. 21-25.
4. *C.D.*, IV/l, pp. 128-138.
5. Cf. *Karl Barth's Table Talk.* Recorded and edited by John D. Godsey, *Scottish Journal of Theology Occasional Papers* No. 10, Edinburgh: Oliver & Boyd, 1963; pp. 1-3. Godsey entitles his article 'The Architecture of Karl Barth's *Church Dogmatics.*" By this he means that the structuring of the work seeks to reflect the imprint of God's revelation and so is a trinitarian structure. He writes "Here we do not find the Loci-scheme of Melanchthon and most old orthodox dogmatics or the credal formulation of Calvin or the inductive logic of Schleiermacher, but a willingness to follow the structural lines of the revelation itself. That is, the architecture bears the impress of God's revelation to his Church in the Lord Jesus Christ." Ibid., p. 3.
6. *C.D.*, IV/l pp. 358ff.
7. *C.D.*, IV/2, pp. 378ff.
8. *C.D.*, IV/3,1, pp. 368ff.
9. *C.D.*, IV/l, p. 138.
10. Ibid., pp. 157ff.
11. Ibid., pp. 211-283.
12. Ibld., pp. 301ff.
13. Ibid.

14. Ibid., p. 303 own translation.

15. Ibid., p. 301.

16. Ibid., p. 304.

17. *C.D.*, III/2, p. 448.

18. R. Bultmann, "New Testament and Mythology" in *Kerygma and Myth*, Vol.. 1, H. W. Bartsch, ed., trs. R. H. Fuller, London: S.P.C.K. 1953, p. 41. For Bultmann the resurrection simply reveals the significance of the cross and is not a new act of God. He writes in a much disputed passage *"Faith in the resurrection is really the same thing as faith in the saving efficacy of the cross, faith in the cross as the cross of Christ."* Ibid., p. 41.

19. Ibid., pp. 40, 42.

20. Ibid., 38f. T. F. Torrance, *Space, Time and Resurrection*, Edinburgh: The Handsel Press, 1976 deals with this aspect also but gives little attention to the Holy Spirit.

21., See *C.D.*, IV/1, pp. 283ff. The Verdict of the Father. Here Rosato (*The Spirit as Lord*, p. 109f) cannot be followed in making pneumatology the "dominant theme" of the *Church Dogmatics* (Vol IV).

22. *C.D.*, IV/2, pp. 302ff., 319ff.

23. *C.D.*, IV/3, 1, p. 350.

24. Ibid., p. 350.

25. *C.D.*, IV/2, pp. 341-360. This is worked out in more detail by Thompson in "On the Trinity" in *Theology Beyond Christendom*, 1986, pp. 13-31.

26. Ibid., pp. 360-377.

27. Berthold Klappert, *Die Auferweckung des Gekreuzigten, Der Ansatz der Christologie Karl Barths in Zusammenhang der Christologie der Gegenwart*. Neukirchener Verlag, 1971, pp. 187-188.

28. John V. Taylor, *The Go-Between God*, London: S.C.M., 1972.

29. *C.D.*, IV/2, p. 318.

30. For the following see the original essay of Bultmann "New Testament and Mythology", in *Kerygma and Myth*, op.cit., pp. 1-44.

31. Ibid., p. 36.

32. *C.D.*, IV/3, 1, p. 350.

33. Karl Barth, Rudolf Bultmann; An Attempt to Understand Him, *Kerygma and Myth*, Volume II, ed. Hans Werner Bartsch; trs. Reginald H. Fuller, London: S.P.C.K., 1962, p. 10.

34. *C.D.*, IV/3, 1, p. 349.

35. The same objection, in a slightly different form and context, can be made against Roman Catholicism. Here it is the "sacramentally endowed vicars" who are the "other Christs", who threaten in some measure to set limits to Christ's activity.

CHAPTER SIX

THE HOLY SPIRIT AND THE CHURCH

In the theology of Karl Barth, the reconciliation of the world in Christ and the nature of the Church are closely interrelated. He writes: "The history of Jesus Christ is the history of the reconciliation of the world with God."[1] Christ as Reconciler of the world, is both Head and King of the race and at the same time Head and King of the Church; thus his rule is wider than the sphere of the Church. Yet the Church is the provisional form of what in reality has happened to and for the world; it is the provisional form of reconciliation. It has its basis in Christ who is the Reconciler of all and Head of all but who is acknowledged only in the Church; hence there is implicit in this outreach to all in mission and service to the Lord of all and for all.

In becoming incarnate and reconciling sinful humanity to himself God has established an ontological connexion with all humanity through Jesus Christ."This insight is the germ of Barth's ecclesiology, whose main purpose is to show how the objective reconciliation of all men in Jesus Christ takes on concrete form when Christians recognise and proclaim the real union between their existence and that of their Lord."[2]

In entering this area we are not leaving behind the creedal or christological basis but maintaining it . Here we are dealing with the "active participation of man in the divine act of reconciliation."[3] It is the subjective side of the one act of reconciliation which, on the basis of the objective, comes again to the fore at this point. Here is the place where it happens that, by the Holy Spirit, humanity shares

in the work of Christ and a Church, a community of faith is
created. Here Barth can speak in a way reminiscent of Roman Catholic theology of our participation in God' s reconciliation. The meaning is, however, significantly different
in that, for Barth, humanity does not co-operate with grace
but becomes a subject by God's act alone.

But what is the Church? Basing his thoughts primarily on all that Christ is and has done and taking particular account of 1 Corinthians 12:12 Barth can first of all
identify the Church with Jesus Christ himself.[4] As the
Church is one body and has many members so also is
Christ. He is the Body. Barth speaks of two forms of the
body of Christ: the heavenly historical form as exalted Lord
and at the same time the earthly historical form as the
Church on earth. One can put it in this way. As the body
crucified and risen Christ includes the Church within himself and his action in reconciliation—that is the heavenly
historical form. In reality there is only one body of Christ
with two forms and there are three stages in this whole activity as Barth sees it;[5]

a) election from all eternity of the Church in and
with Christ;

b) its realization in time in the incarnation, cross
and resurrection; and

c) its visible appearance by the Holy Spirit as an
historical comrnunity.

Barth writes, "The Holy Spirit is the power, and his
action the work of the co-ordination of the being of Jesus
Christ and that of his community as distinct from and yet
enclosed within it. Just as the Holy Spirit, as himself an
eternal divine "person" or mode of being, as the Spirit of
the Father and the Son (*qui ex Patre Filioque procedit*), is
the bond of peace between the two, so in the historical
work of reconciliation he is the One who constitutes and
guarantees the unity of the *totus Christus*, i.e., of Jesus
Christ in the heights and in the depths, in his transcendence
and in his immanence . . . He is the One who constitutes
and guarantees the unity in which he is at one and the same

time the heavenly Head with God and the earthly body with his community."[6] At the same time this community is the result of the will and purpose of God in election. "The Holy Spirit creates in the Church a community whose existence in fact corresponds to the divine election of all men in Jesus Christ. The ecclesial community is thus introduced by the Holy Spirit into nothing less than the eternal obedience of God's Word."[7] Just as the Son obeys the Father in becoming incarnate, choosing humanity and including us in this so we, by the Holy Spirit, communally and personally are enabled to share in this self-surrender and obedience.

Here again in a profound way in ecclesiology the doctrines of the Trinity, election, reconciliation and pneumatology are brought together.[8] Here too Barth speaks of the Spirit in his mediating role uniting, as it were, Christ in the height and in the depth, as heavenly Head and earthly body, as one *totus Christus.*

It is important to remember that Barth's doctrine of the Church comes within his large volumes on the doctrine of reconciliation. Just as there are three aspects to reconciliation the Son humbling himself to do his priestly work, humanity being exalted through the Son to a royal office, and the Son as the God-man being his own self-witness—the light and truth of the world—so there are three aspects of the Church corresponding to these. Here we see again the consistent symmetry and architectonic of Barth's thought and dogmatics:

Corresponding to God the Son in obedience, humbling himself to death in his priestly work, the Church is called and gathered by him:[9]

Corresponding to humanity exalted to fellowship with God, to kingship, the Church is built up and grows up into Christ:[10]

Corresponding to the prophetic work, the God-man, the self-witness of Jesus Christ as light and life, the community of faith is sent into the world to bear witness to Christ as Lord and victor, to be a missionary agent of his light in the darkness.[11]

A. THE HOLY SPIRIT AND THE AWAKENING OF THE COMMUNITY

In the sphere of the Church we are in the sphere of the work of the Holy Spirit. We are in the realm of the third article, *credo in spiritum sanctum, credo ecclesiam* I believe in the Holy Spirit, I believe the Church. Why is this so? Because, while we are speaking of human experience, action, faith and community, it is not of something that we can create or realize by our own capacity but (quoting Luther) Barth can say, "The Holy Spirit has called me by the Gospel, enlightened me with his gifts, sanctified and maintained me in a right faith as he calls and gathers and enlightens the whole of Christendom, keeping it to Jesus Christ in the true and only faith."[12] Sinful humanity is incapable of awakening itself to the life of Christ and needs "a particular awakening power of God, by which he is born again to this will and ability, to the freedom of this action . . . God in this awakening power, God as the Creator of this other man, is the Holy Spirit."[13] That a person—a wholly unworthy, incapable sinner—is given this capacity, the freedom to believe, to know this new life in the fellowship of Christ and his people is a real miracle of grace. The reconciliation of the world with God in Christ is now by the Spirit our own reconciliation with God.

Yet while the Spirit makes us free, it does not become the possession of the Church or under our control. The Spirit is and remains the free Lord in its action in us. But how do we know this true Holy Spirit from false spirits? Barth's basic answer is that it attests Jesus Christ as Lord. He puts this in two ways,

a)"The Holy Spirit is clearly marked off from these spirits by the fact that he is the Spirit of God who acts in Jesus Christ, reconciling the world to himself and revealing himself in the world as the doer of this work."[14]

b) He adds to this first point by saying that Jesus Christ attests his own reconciliation to us and does so by the Spirit. The true Holy Spirit is the one who is the agent of this. "He is the power in which Jesus Christ attests himself, attests himself effectively, creating in man response and obedience."[15] And as Jesus Christ awakens us to life for himself he unites us with himself and with one another. The Church is the one, holy catholic and apostolic Church. It is "the living community of the living Lord Jesus Christ in the fulfilment of its existence."[16] That is, it is a divine society called into being by God the Holy Spirit.

Fundamentally the Holy Spirit is in this sense the subjective reality of reconciliation or atonement. It is the power of Jesus Christ in which Christ becomes ours and we become his in a living community of faith. It is God and humanity together in this way as community that is the Church and this is due to the power of the Holy Spirit awakening dead sinners to living faith and obedience. The "how" of this is God's mystery and is not open to us to know.

Three further things (among many) may be said of the Church and the Spirit at this point.[17]

First, the Church gathered together by the Word and Spirit as a community of Jesus Christ has always an *event* character. By this Barth means that the Holy Spirit is the Lord who comes again and again to make us anew. The Spirit is not identical with the Church or its soul as is the view of Catholicism. That the Spirit is given to it does not detract from its Lordship or transcendence over the Church. Again it means that the Church exists always in a relationship of obedience to the sovereignty of Jesus Christ, responding actively to his Word, work and will. It is a living, dynamic community. Barth can even speak of it as a history that takes place between God and certain people. Its being is in its activity, in this calling and gathering by the Holy Spirit. One can indeed speak not only of the *event* character but also of the "being" of the Church. We, by putting on Christ, experience a renewal of our being—a change noetically corresponding to that wrought in our humanity ontically by the union of God and humanity in Jesus Christ. The revolutionary change that happened in our humanity in

Christ altering the whole relationship between God and us
has now become concrete and actual in the Christian community. The Church's "being" is in this "becoming" again
and again by Word and Spirit. It is one with Christ in his
being and action by the Holy Spirit.

Secondly, the Church exists as *visible* and *invisible*.
The Reformers and later Protestant dogmatics made such a
distinction clearly to counter the claims of the Roman Catholic Church of the day, yet also in the succession of Augustine. The invisible Church was the community of all the
elect, past, present and to come, whereas the visible was the
number of those actually within the Church on earth pro-
fessing the true faith. This may be a possible deduction
from the New Testament but it is never explicitly so stated
there.

Barth, however, goes a somewhat different way
when he uses these words. Its invisibility points to its secret
hidden source in God the Holy Spirit. Just as Jesus the Son
came veiled in the lowliness of our humanity, so the greatness of the Church is in its invisible origin and continuous
power. But just as the Word made flesh came for our salvation so the Spirit presses out to create a visible community
in the world and for the world. Its visibility in concrete
form is a necessary aspect of its being and there is to be no
ecclesiastical docetism.

Thirdly, the Church has before it the word *credo*—
not I believe in the Church as one believes in God or in Jesus Christ, but I perceive by faith that God by his Spirit is
at work here. To know the Church simply externally is
largely to misunderstand it as is often done by the average
statesman, politician or journalist. It can thus only properly
be understood from within. True, its spiritual character can
be seen in manifestations and analogies in its visible form
but its true, spiritual nature is God's doing and can only be
believed. Yet it must be again underlined that "no concrete
form of the community can in itself and as such be the object of faith."[18] To believe the Church is to believe in the
Lord of the Church.

Barth agrees with the *Catechismus Romanus,* the Roman Catechism, that we know by faith alone: *fide solum intelligimus,* but he is critical of the Encyclical of Pope Pius XII *Mystici Corporis* (1943) where there seems to be, as Barth puts it, "an unconditional identification of the mystery of the Church as created and maintained and ruled by Christ through the Holy Spirit with its historical action and judicial organisation . . . It itself is always right in everything. What the Church is is not hidden. It does not need to be believed. It can be directly deduced from what the Church is and does as the visible Church, from the excellence of its existence as it may be seen by all. But why call it 'mystical' if it can be perceived directly without any difficulty?"[19] He adds, however, "We must not overlook the fact that within modern Roman Catholicism there are those who think and speak of the Church in a way which is very different and which seems to give fresh life to the *fide solum intelligimus,* cf. the stimulating writing of H. U. von Balthasar (*Geschleifte Bastionen*) and F. Heer (*Das Experiment Europa*)."[20] No doubt Vatican II took a further step and a similar line in the new direction von Balthasar and others were taking and Barth welcomes this also. Yet this only goes part of the necessary way. "At the beginning of everything, beclouding everything stands the dogma summarised and proclaimed in the first Vatican Council concerning the prolongation of the office of Peter in each bearer of the papal crown and the infallibility of his judgement in matters of doctrine and life when he speaks *ex cathedra* (with or without the agreement of the other bishops or the rest of the Church altogether)."[21] The view that the Church is infallible as this is centered in the Pope is for Barth a wholly unacceptable one and gives a conception of it which he cannot share.

More positively Barth points also to common elements in the Catholic ecumenical and in the non-Roman Catholic ecumenical movements as follows: "Both are directed to the unification of all Christianity as their final end. Both live by the dynamics of the evangelical Word

and Spirit which are totally constitutive for both. Both live
to the extent that they are living communities of the living
Jesus Christ."[22] And, as he adds, both are confronted with
and called to attend, to follow and obey the movement of
God in Christ by the Spirit.

B. THE HOLY SPIRIT AND THE UPBUILDING OF THE
    COMMUNITY

        Just as the human Jesus is lifted up and we with him
to union and fellowship with God and to holiness of life, so
the Church, his body is caught up and carried in its life and
service in the same direction. This is the sanctification of
the Church and this sanctification is but the provisional representation of that of all humanity and human life as it has
taken place in Jesus Christ. The Church "continues and is
only as he sanctifies men and their human work, building
up them and their work into the true Church. He does this,
however, in the time between the resurrection and the return of Jesus Christ and therefore in the time of the community."[23] Here Barth is speaking of the Holy Spirit. He has always in mind three things, the act of God in Christ which is
all inclusive, our incorporation into this movement and action and the inevitable thrust outwards to embrace the cosmic sphere of the world and all men.
        This threefold thrust reveals again the ontological
connexion between Christ, the community and the world. It
is, as we have seen, not only a matter of action but of being.
The being of Jesus Christ which includes all humanity in
reconciliation has its analogy in the Christian community
when the Spirit brings people into actual and active communion with the Lord and with one another. But this being
of the community prospectively involves all who are included under the Lordship of Christ. Here an ontological
connexion links Christ, community and world in an inclusive christology, a fellowship gathered and built up by
Christ and missionary obligation to the world. This is in
fact a summation of Barth's christological—ecclesiological,

theological ontology and dynamic.

The Church, however, according to Barth, is to be seen in three main ways,[24]

a) As a community that is built up as a temple of God by the Spirit. It is God in Christ by the Spirit who is the builder (Matt. 16:18; 1 Peter 2:4). "Let yourselves be built as living stones into a spiritual temple." Paradoxically it is at the same time our work (1 Cor. 3:9); we are God's fellow workers. We work because he works in and through us. This takes place primarily, according to Barth, where the Church is met for worship. Paul uses the word *oikodome* most frequently when he speaks of the Church, the congregation gathered for worship. There it learns together and is built up in the faith.

b) The Church also grows up into Christ, growing up as it were into the reality it has and is in him. Its growth is both extensive moving out and expanding, but, more particularly, it is intensive growth in holiness and fellowship. For it is the communion of saints, *communion* in the *Holy Spirit*, "These men—the saints—who live and act in the communion of the one Holy Spirit, and therefore in communion one with another, are Christians."[25] The Church is the communion of the *sancti*, the saints, that is, of those who are sanctified by the Holy Spirit, of all Christians of every age and place, the *communio sanctorum*..

While the community always remains imperfect, weak and vulnerable, yet by the power of the Spirit its growth is always new and astonishing. For it reflects the reality, history and movement of Jesus Christ. It lives and grows and is because and as Jesus lives. Barth always underlines the fact that the work of the Spirit in building up the Church in holiness, as in all else, is a history, bringing the living Lord Jesus Christ to us and us to him. In the Holy Spirit Jesus Christ attests himself as the crucified and risen One and exalts us in him. He causes the community to grow by the Holy Spirit.

c) The Church is maintained and upheld in the world by the same risen Lord present by the Spirit. Barth

would scarcely subscribe to the claim that the presence of
the Holy Spirit guarantees infallible truth, but he does see
the Church guided and guarded by the Spirit when tempted
by the twin dangers of secularism, secularization (worldli-
ness) and self-glorification (sacralisation)—triumphalism.
To compromise with the world is to "relax its relationship
to the Holy Spirit and his gifts,"[26] to glorify one's own self
means "its own common spirit replaces the Holy Spirit, and
its own work the work of God."[27] But to be upheld by the
Spirit means that despite our failures and weaknesses we
can avoid these dangers and, if we are enabled to do so, the
paradox will again be seen, "The destructable cannot in fact
be destroyed." This means that the truth of its being is
maintained by Christ, by the Spirit and not by us.

One question which it is right to ask in connection
with the Holy Spirit, his work and gifts in and to the
Church is this: does Barth see any merit in, or has he anything to say about, the charismatic movement, the so-called
charismata in the Church? There is little specific reference
but he does point out that the one Holy Spirit gives a variety of gifts to the Church. He does continually speak of the
Church being set in motion and kept in motion by the Holy
Spirit, of the living Lord giving growth and dynamic for
new insights and conclusions. There is always the dynamic
from above and not from social and political changes and
revolutions and in only one place known to me does he explicitly mention these gifts and that is in *The Faith of the
Church*, which is the French edition of his commentary on
the Apostles' Creed.

On one occasion when questioned about the fruits
of the Spirit Barth replied in a twofold way;

First, these "special manifestations—speaking in
tongues, healing of sicknesses, etc. they are possible conse-
quences of the gift of the Holy Spirit. They could not be
conditions which alone authorize those who meet them to
decide that they possess the Holy Spirit."[28] In other words
they certainly are to be interpreted as such gifts but are not
to be seen as indispensable preconditions, verifications or

tests of the presence of the Spirit. Barth regards the cross and resurrection seen as the consummation of Christ's life and of God's eternal purpose as the'"bread", the indispensable central element of the Gospel. To this must be added the work of the Holy Spirit in making this real to us and in us. The other he calls "cake". Let us receive the bread of life and then "for dessert perhaps, we shall receive all these delicacies."[29]

Secondly, Barth asks if we do not already have all the extraordinary things God wills for us in the Word and sacraments. Certainly, to envisage special gifts for an elite, intended "for special Christians, particular gifts pretended to be indispensable to some state of perfection" is to go beyond what is set out in the Word of God. Barth, however, with typical openness to receive truth and light from any quarter, says, "if all those who advocate these special manifestations want to be heard in the Church, let them show them to her and, then, I hope that the whole Church will be capable of obeying the voice of truth."[31]

In the *Church Dogmatics* Barth does recognise clearly "the freedom of varied movements in the sphere of the one and manifold Spirit and his gift and gifts given to them."[32] The Spirit is Lord and sovereign and so works in great freedom but also in great variety. At the same time in and with this rich variety the Holy Spirit creates unity and gives to each as it wills. The Spirit has as such a particular will for each Christian. "All differences in the community rest on the variety of his distribution."[33] The community itself is pneumatic and is strong and healthy as it gives free rein to the Holy Spirit.

C. THE HOLY SPIRIT AND THE SENDING OF THE COMMUNITY

We saw how in the doctrine of reconciliation there are the three movements of God; the third is the outward movement as the Word and Truth attesting the total movement of reconciliation. Jesus Christ is the content and meaning of all three and as we now look at this third aspect we see that he attests himself as the truth and light of the world. He does so in and through his community; here we see Barth's cosmic survey, his missionary outreach and the dynamic power of his thought at its clearest. For Jesus Christ is his own self-witness by the Holy Spirit, and in and through the community he reaches out in his truth and light to the world already his *de jure* (by right) by reconciliation. It is not yet *de facto* (actually) his but presses towards this consummation.

The community in which Christ dwells yet over which he is Lord, which is one with him, built up into him, is also his instrument in and for the world. A new and fresh understanding of the world is given to the Church by the Holy Spirit. It sees the world as one addressed by the free grace of God in Jesus Christ and it sees Jesus Christ as the one who in himself and of himself is the radical alteration of the world. Reconciliation is God's revolution, his change of the world to a right relationship with himself. Since this is so, the community has this realistic knowledge of the world in the light of grace. Since Jesus Christ identified himself with us in our need and sinfulness the Church will know a total solidarity with the world, and since he took its concerns to himself, his community will live in active responsibility in and for the world.[34]

So the Church as the living community of Jesus Christ exists in and for the world. The Holy Spirit of the living Christ reaches out to all or, as Barth puts it, Jesus Christ in his prophetic Word and action reveals his grace to men through the Church and enables them to receive the Word of his work. Thus the very nature of the Church is a missionary one, based on the triune God, on Christ's reconciliation and its revelation as truth and light and on the power of the Spirit bringing it in enabling efficacy to humanity.

At the same time the Spirit manifests Jesus as Victor by his superior power. Jesus both reveals and overcomes the adversary in his true nature. There is a teleology of the Spirit's work in a continual but victorious conflict with the Evil One. This victory the Spirit effects by its presence in the Church reaching out in grace and mission to all.

In speaking of mission Barth sets out clearly in six points what he regards as the conditions of true missionary activity.[35]

a) The presupposition that everything has already been done for men and women in the world, that is in reconciliation in Jesus Chrlst.

b) Mission is not an optional work or the preserve of a few nor simply the task of missionary societies but is the task of the Church as a whole. True, only individuals can act as missionaries to go abroad but the Church as a whole should be missionary in outlook.

c) The sole purpose of mission is the proclamation of the Gospel and the conversion of men and women to Christ and not the strengthening, confirmation or extension of Western or any other culture, civilization or politics. In the past the faith followed the flag and there were established little colonies not only of Christians but of Presbyterians and Methodists and Catholics in India, for example. It was then discovered that the Indians might believe in Christ but our denominational and cultural habits were and are largely alien to them; hence we have attempts at and actual unions in North and South India.

d) On the human level mission should be carried out with the greatest respect for the values in other religions, but with a sincere lack of respect for them from the point of view of the Gospel. The Gospel must be opposed both to theism and these religions in all its uniqueness and novelty with no attempt to compromise or water down its truth, but offered in the spirit and reality of love.

e) Mission involves the whole person and so a care for humans in their totality. Education, healing, help and the needs of all have rightly been associated with mission though never its main goal.

f) The goal of missionary work is to make a missionary Church, to attest to the nations the God who wills to make them too his witnesses and missionaries.

Finally, Barth does not believe in mission to the Jews because he regards them as standing in a special relationship to the Gospel and in his exposition of Romans 9-11 he makes this quite clear. Yet, while dialogue is important and necessary, it is doubtful whether one can exclude altogether the missionary thrust in this direction too. But the main purpose of missionary work is to enable others themselves to become the community of faith and so do the work God has sent the Church into the world to do. It is to be, therefore, a witness (and witness is one of the words which Barth uses very frequently, especially in his later writings), a testimony to Christ more than to our experience of him.

Here we have a great vision of the Church as called, as built up and as sent by Jesus Christ into the world to be his body, to be his instrument in his saving and loving purpose for all. As such, it is purely the representative forerunner of what he has done for and wills to do for the world.

The view that all are included in Christ's reconciliation objectively has been criticised by some as a form of objectivism.[36] This is, however, an unacceptable criticism since it misses the point of Christ's representative humanity involving an inclusive christology. Nor can the objection be sustained that Barth's idea of evangelism is a mere announcement without persuasion.[37] To be a true witness, in Barth's understanding, is to speak in the persuasive power of the Holy Spirit.

Another aspect of Barth's thought which is sometimes missed is that witness involves testimony to Jesus Christ who is Lord of all. This means affirming the need for personal salvation and communal life, but also speaking a word to the social and political problems of the day. Barth strongly affirmed this as an important and indispensable aspect of the community's total witness to Christ. To make the social and political the determinative aspect as is the tendency of F. W. Marquardt[38] or to ignore it, as many do, is to misunderstand Barth's whole christology and ecclesiology. Ulrich Dannemann has pointed out[39] that in the relationship between theology and politics in Barth there is what he calls both a *Wort zur Sache* and also a *Wort zur Lage*. By the former he means the content of the Christian revelation and by the latter the necessary word which the former speaks to specific situations and needs, for example Nazism.

Barth is, in fact saying that the task of the community in the power of the Spirit is to be a witness to Christ, to bring men and women into the community through a living faith in the crucified and risen Lord Jesus Christ. But this central aspect must not be proclaimed or pursued as an end in itself or seen as a timeless truth in abstraction from the world. The *Wort zur Sache* is a word relevant and powerful in a world *de jure* Christ's by reconciliation. Barth writes, "There can be no doubt that, when its relevance to specific times and situations is taken from it, intentionally or unintentionally the Gospel is no longer preached as the declaration of the risen Christ who rules at the right hand of the Father Almighty but who also by his Holy Spirit lives and acts and speaks in the ongoing earthly and temporal history of the world and the Church."[40] The Holy Spirit is the active (one could say the ontic) power of God in the concrete situations of the world leading the community not only to know the power of Christ as Lord but to waken from neutrality to active involvement with a word and work for social and political issues. At the same time Barth warned against the danger of adapting the faith to current social, political or cultural conditions and so losing its identity. In fact his position could be well summed up in Moltmann's terms, namely, the proper relationship between *Identity* and *Relevance*,[41] though Barth would not fully share the views of Moltmann later in the same book. His position is a reiteration of the wellknown phrase from his earlier days—"to have the Bible in the one hand and the daily newspaper in the other". It could also be summed up in the words of Visser t'Hooft at Uppsala: "A Christianity which has lost its vertical dimension has lost its salt and is not only insipid in itself, but useless for the world. But a Christianity which would use the vertical preoccupation as a means to escape from its responsibilities for and in the common life of man is a denial of the incarnation, of God's love for the world manifested in Christ."[42]

It is the living Lord Jesus Christ in the power of the Spirit who speaks his prophetic Word in and to the world, calling his fellowship to faith and mission but also to active concern for righteousness, peace and freedom in social and political life. Because the Spirit is active in this way it is therefore incorrect for Rosato to say that Barth has no ontic role for the Spirit and that Barth's active political engagement is not matched by his theology.[43] Hendrikus Berkhof has countered this effectively by pointing out that the Spirit in the earlier writings of Barth has a purely subjective, noetic role but that later there is a widening of vision to see the Spirit in a more active way, doing its own distinctive work, yet never divorced from the living Lord. The Spirit is the power of the risen Christ reaching out to all, powerful in mission and in liberation. Berkhof writes, "To the best of my knowledge in the handbooks of dogmatics only Barth has thoroughly done justice to this comprehensive vision, in the last of his three perspectives."[44] Here "the Spirit (is) the power of Christ's resurrection, which works the miracles of light, liberation, knowledge, peace, and life (even healing)."[45]

The community created by the prophetic Word in the power of the Spirit is not an end in itself but a witness to the world. It is as the *communio sanctorum* also "*a coniuratio testium*, the confederation of the witnesses who may and must speak because they believe. The community does not speak with words alone. It speaks by the very fact of its existence in the world; by its characteristic attitude to world problems; and, moreover and especially, by its silent service to all the handicapped, weak, and needy in the world. It speaks, finally, by the simple fact that it prays for the world. It does all this because this is the purpose of its summons by the Word of God. It cannot avoid doing these things, since it believes."[46]

D. COMMENT AND EVALUATION OF BARTH ON THE CHURCH

There are certain very notable features and strengths in Barth's lengthy exposition of the Holy Spirit and the Church.

a) While the Church is the work of the Holy Spirit it is christologically based. The strong emphasis Barth gives to the Church as the body of Christ is itself proof of this. Some have criticised the use of the body metaphor (if such it is) as being used in a much more limited way in the New Testament than is usually imagined.[47] It is by no means the only expression used by the New Testament or by Barth, but it is perhaps more clearly in accord with the total sweep of New Testament teaching and with the nature of the incarnation in particular. No other term has its comprehensive, inclusive nature; indeed with no other is the Church identified with Christ.[48]

b) Barth gives priority to the Church as the creation of the Holy Spirit over the individual who is brought to new life within the sphere of the Church. Calvin followed the order—the Spirit, the individual, and the Church but did not thereby intend any minimizing of the place of the Church as the mother of us all. Later Protestantism tended to see the work of the Spirit as first related to the individual and then to the Church.

H. Berkhof[49] speaks of Barth as manifesting a duality and as typical of the Reformed position which wanted to see the Spirit in relation to the individual but recognised the Church as the creation of God. This is not, however, Barth's position; he is, in fact, with Berkhof in maintaining the logical and theological priority of the Church over the individual as the sequence of his exposition shows.

c) One of the most stimulating and original aspects of Barth's doctrine is the basis that he gives for the missionary task of the Church. Christ is seen as the prophet who declares by the Spirit his own reconciliation of the world. This insight and theological interpretation of the missionary

basis and nature of the work of the Spirit in Christ's prophetic office is an impressive feature of his exposition. The
Spirit is not just the power of Christ's resurrection regener-
ating within the Church and building up its members to
grow in sanctification, but is the power reaching out
through the Church to the world and the whole created cosmos. The Spirit is in a sense the risen Christ as prophet declaring his work and reaching out to claim all and all humanity to his allegiance.

Berkhof regrets the lack of integration in the past
between missionary work and official theology. Dogmatic
theology has thus largely failed to give a proper theological
basis for missionary work. Berkhof, however, adds, "there
is one great exception, however: Barth's *Church Dogmatics*
IV,3 . . . the highly original and fruitful composition of Vol.
IV in general, and the way in which Barth treats the whole
of theology under the missionary aspect in IV/3 have yet to
find the attention they deserve."[50]

d) There is also in this section a strong combination
of ontology (Being) and dynamic (action). This is typical of
Barth's whole theology and goes back to his conception of
God as a Being in action. Neither one aspect nor the other
can be seen or understood in isolation. The Church owes its
being to the continual event of its becoming by Word and
Spirit. The being of the Church is in the very being of Jesus
Christ in his action in reconciliation. By the Spirit we are
incorporated into him and share in his life. We continually
become what we already are in him. There is a reality,
movement and life in the Christian community which it
owes to its continual renewal by the Holy Spirit. This is the
answer to the charge sometimes made against Barth that being and continuity are lost in the ever renewed event character of his thought. What he is concerned to preserve is the
truth that *God* as he *is* in Christ is *active* here; he is, however, at work not as the immanent truth of the Church but as
its Lord.

Nor can it be argued that Barth's affirmation of the
Church as the *totus Christus* is an approximation to those

who hold that the Church is the extension of the incarnation. The Church by the Spirit does not extend Christ's being and work but is united with him and commissioned to serve and witness to him in the whole of life.

There are, however, two interrelated aspects where possibly less than justice has been done by Barth to certain biblical insights. The first is in relation to Christ as High Priest—though his writing may imply this. As risen and exalted Lord he is High Priest and continues by the Spirit to exercise a service to humanity as he did in the days of his flesh. In this function he not only calls, equips and sends the Church to minister, to serve him in the world but he also calls particular individuals to special ministries. Barth's lack of emphasis on Christ as High Priest and on the institutional aspect combined with his strong emphasis on community leads to a strange lack of mention of the ministry as we generally understand it, and of ordination in particular. Clearly Barth believes in the ministry but it is particularly "the community as a fellowship of ministry and witness."[51] There is also little emphasis on preaching though this is a central aspect in Barth's theology as a whole. Presumably it is the community that decides who is to represent it and ordination is simply a matter of proper "ordering".

This criticism of an apparent lack in no way takes away from what is an enriching exposition including a great variety of diverse gifts of service by the one Spirit.[52]

Secondly, Barth is critical of what was and is sometimes called Jewish mission.[53] There is both truth and danger in this position.

God manifest in Christ is the God of Israel; hence we do not relate to the Jews as we do to those who know little or nothing of the true God. The people of Israel continue to be the chosen of God for his calling and gifts are irrevocable. But since the chosen people "at the decisive moment . . . denied its election and calling" Barth asks, "Can there ever be a true conversion of true Jews . . . except as a highly extraordinary event?"[55] One would have thought that this would have meant mission to them as the instruments of God. No, says Barth, our duty is, to use Paul's phrase, to "make the synagogue jealous ."[56] The Church should itself be a testimony to grace and set this before the eyes of the Jews to provoke them to desire the same way and life. This is itself a form of witness very close to mission.

It is thus partly a matter of terminology since Barth uses mission almost exclusively in relation to the Gentiles (as does Vatican II), and uses witness as a more general term. Clearly in the latter sense Barth is not against but in favour of making the central Christian affirmation that Jesus the Messiah, the King of the Jews is the Saviour of the world and the Jewish Saviour too. Yet, strangely for Barth, to the Jew one must show this in life and action; to the Gentile both show and declare it. But why not both to each of these groups? Did not Paul say "To the Jew first," and did not the early Church proclaim to the Jews that Jesus was their Messiah and Lord? Nevertheless Barth's approach reminds us of the complexities of any exegesis of Romans 9-11, with its pointer to the particular role of Israel and the need for special understanding for this reason.

NOTES

1 *C.D.*, IV/l, p. 644.

2. Rosato, *The Spirit as Lord*, p. 123.

3. *C.D.*, IV/l, p. 643.

4. Ibid., p. 663.

5. Ibid., p. 667.

6. *C.D.*, IV/3, 2, p. 760.

7. Rosato, op.cit., p. 67.

8. Cf. the perceptive way Colin O'Grady has structured his first book *The Church in the Theology of Karl Barth*, Vol. I, London: Geoffrey Chapman, 1970 in summarizing Barth's doctrine of the Church. He sees and sets out the underlying trinitarian, predestinarian and christological nature of Barth's treatment. He sets it out as follows: Section One. The Church of God; The Eternal Basis of the Church in

God's Election of Grace (Ibid., pp. 100ff.). Section Two. The Church in the Son: The Objective Realization of Reconciliation (Ibid., pp. 130ff.). Section Three. The Church through the Holy Spirit: The Fundamental Form of the Subjective Realization of Reconciliation. (Ibid., pp. 172ff.). O'Grady thus shows that a trinitarian structure and basis is found in the whole texture and content of the *Church Dogmatics*. The Trinity is not incidental to, but is an integral aspect of all theology.

9. *C.D.*, IV/1, pp. 643ff.
10. *C.D.*, IV/2, pp. 641ff.
11. *C.D.*, IV/3, 2. pp. 681ff.
12. *C.D.*, IV/1, p. 645.
13. Ibid.
14. Ibid., p. 647; cf. C.D., IV/2, pp. 323-330 for a fuller exposition of the nature of the holiness of the Spirit.
15. Ibid., p. 648.
16. Ibid., p. 652.
17. Ibid., pp. 650f.
18. Ibid., p. 658.
19. Ibid., p. 659.
20. Ibid.
21. Karl Barth *Ad Limina Apostolorum*, trs. Keith R. Crim, Edinburgh: The Saint Andrews Press, p. 71.
22. Ibid., pp. 72-73.
23. *C.D.*, IV/2, p. 617.
24. Ibid., pp. 623ff.
25. Ibid., p. 642.
26. Ibid., p. 666.
27. Ibid., p. 669.
28. Karl Barth, *The Faith of the Church, A Commentary on the Apostles' Creed*, trs. Gabriel Vahanian, London: Fontana Books, 1958, p. 112. Since Barth's writings the charismatic movement had grown considerably with a wealth of literature. For a good summary of the church's considered response see *The Church is Charismatic, The World Council of Churches and the Charismatic Renewal*. ed., Arnold Bettlinger, Geneva: World Council of Churches, 1981.
29. Ibid.
30. Ibid.
31. Ibid.
32. *C.D.*, IV/1, p. 667. Barth's sympathetic evaluation of the

work of Christoph Blumhardt in *Protestant Theology in the Nineteenth Century*, Valley Forge: Judson Press, 1972, pp. 643-654, shows an openness to Spirit-inspired movements and hopes. Moreover, the title of a section of the *Church Dogmatics*, IV/3,1, pp. 165ff is taken directly from an experience of a girl said to be demon-possessed and cured by divine healing at Blumhardt's church. On recovery she uttered the words "Jesus is Victor." i.e. Victor by the Holy Spirit over all the opposing evil forces.

33. *C.D.*, IV/2, p. 321. Cf. C.D., IV/3, 2, pp. 856-859.

34. *C.D.*, IV/3, 2, pp. 763ff.

35. Ibid., pp. 824, 874-876.

36. Waldron Scott, *Karl Barth's Theology of Mission*. Outreach and Identity: Evangelical Theological Monographs, No. I, Exeter: The Paternoster Press, 1978, p.40. Cf. J. Lesslie Newbigin, *The Open Secret*, Grand Rapids: Eerdmans, 1981.

37. Ibid.

38. F. W. Marquardt. *Theologie und Sozialismus, Das Beispiel Karl Barths*, Munich: Chr. Kaiser Verlag, 1972; see also George Hunsinger,"Conclusion: Towards a Radical Barth," in *Karl Barth and Radical Politics*, ed. George Hunsinger, Philadelphia, The Westminster Press, 1976, pp. 181-227 for a similar overemphasis on the influence of politics on Barth's theology.

39 Ulrich Dannemann, *Theologie und Politik im Denken Karl Barths*, Munich: Chr. Kaiser Verlag, 1977, p. 123.

40. *C.D.*, IV/3, 2, p. 816; cf. Barth's particularly sharp reply to the Bekenntnisbewegung's statement "Kein anderes Evangelium,"when they asked for his comment and support. Since it contained no word about current, burning issues like the Vietnam War, the Jewish Question, the Nuclear Bomb etc, Barth regarded it as straining out a gnat and swallowing a camel—a right Pharisaic affair. See *Junge Kirche*, 6/ 1966, pp. 327f. Orlando Costas, *Liberating News: A Theology of Contextual Evangelisation*, Grand Rapids: Eerdmans, 1989 represents a holistic viewpoint similar to Barth's where personal salvation and change in social structures go hand in hand as belonging to the integrity of the faith.

41. Jürgen Moltmann, *The Crucified God*, trs. R. W. Wilson and John Bowden, London: S.C.M. 1973, pp. 7ff.

42. Kenneth Slack, *Uppsala Report*, London: S.C.M. 1968, p. 25.

43. Rosato, op.cit., p . 170.

44. Hendrikus Berkhof, *Christian Faith, An Introduction to the Study of the Faith*, trs. Sierd Woudstra, Grand Rapids, Michigan, 1973, p . 329; cf. also Berkhof, *The Doctrine of the Holy Spirit*, pp. 29 and 90 for further commendation of Barth's view on the place of the Spirit in witness.

45. Berkhof, *The Doctrine of the Holy Spirit*, p . 29 .

46. Barth, *Evangelical Theology*, p. 38.

47. C. F. D. Moule, *The Holy Spirit*, London and Oxford: Mowbrays, 1978, p. 70; cf., however, the significant title of Ernest Best's book, *One Body in Christ*, London: S.P.C.K., 1955, in reference to the Church.

48. See I Cor. 12 :12.

49. Berkhof, *The Doctrine of the Holy Spirit*, p. 49.

50. Ibid., p. 33.

51. *C.D.*, IV/3, 2, p. 868. Barth's view of the Church as a ministering community is close to the Congregationalist view of Church polity and diverges from the Reformed conception of an essentially presbyterial system. T. F. Torrance, "My Interaction with Karl Barth", in *How Karl Barth Changed My Mind*, ed. Donald K. McKim, Grand Rapids: Eerdmans, 1986, p. 62 makes a similar criticism of Barth's supposed lack of emphasis on the Highpriestly work of Christ.

52. Cf. *C.D.*, IV/3, 2, pp. 867-901. Barth indicates twelve forms of service (ministry) given by the Spirit.

53. *C.D.*, IV/3, 2, pp. 876-878.

54. Ibid., p. 877

55. Ibid., p. 878.

56. Ibid.

CHAPTER SEVEN

THE HOLY SPIRIT AND BAPTISM

The traditional teaching of the Churches of the Reformation was and is that there are only two sacraments, namely, Baptism and the Lord's Supper; though it must be added that the incarnation could itself be regarded as the supreme sacrament. The Catholic tradition on the other hand uses the word "sacrament" in three senses: (a) of Jesus Christ himself; (b) of the Church, and (c) of the seven sacraments. The Reformed tradition has largely limited itself to the two central sacraments as especially related to Christ and ordained by him. The meaning of them was, in Calvin's words, "An outward sign by which the Lord seals on our consciences the promises of his good will toward us in order to sustain the weakness of our faith; and we in turn attest our piety toward him in the presence of the Lord, and of his angels and before men."[1] In other words, a sacrament has a twofold purpose, namely God's confirmation of his promises of grace by his Word, and our confession and attestation of faith before God and humanity. As far as baptism was concerned this meant the baptism of infants as well as believers, though no causative or regenerative power was regarded as attached to or coming through the sacrament. Nonetheless sacraments were confirmations of grace, means of grace (to use the most common term).

Karl Barth's attitude towards the sacraments has shown him to be an inheritor of this tradition and yet at the same time to be a critic who rejected certain aspects of it. Probably his earliest teaching on the subject is given in his commentary on Romans as far back as 1922. In this he states clearly that baptism is a sacrament and a means of grace. He writes, "Baptism is a sacrament of truth and holiness" directing us to the word of God." "Baptism mediates the new creation: it is not itself grace, but from first to last a means of grace."[2] This is the traditional teaching of the Reformed Church; the sacrament is a sign and means of grace used by God; it does not operate in a causative way but is a means used by God through his Holy Spirit to bring us his grace. It seems clear that Barth also retained the Reformed teaching on the propriety and right of infant baptism until 1938. The second stage was then reached and found its climax in 1944 when Barth wrote his book, *The Teaching of the Church Regarding Baptism.*[3] Part of the traditional view of Calvin has been retained and part abandonded. Baptism is still a sacrament and means of grace. H. Hartwell writes, "In opposition to Roman, Lutheran and Anglican baptismal teaching Barth then argued that water-baptism as such is not 'a causative or generative means by which there are imparted to man the forgiveness of sins, the Holy Spirit, and even faith—a means by which grace is poured out upon him, so that he is saved and made blessed —a means by which his rebirth is effected,' but aims at man's *cognitio salutis*"[4]—his knowledge of salvation. This means, as Calvin puts it, that baptism's function is to make us aware of the divine grace given and be a means by which we again receive it, but it does not as such regenerate. The real gift of grace comes from Jesus Christ himself and in water baptism man apprehends this and must do so consciously. If this is so it means that the baptism of infants is no longer a valid option. Barth therefore rejected infant baptism. Hartwell again writes "His rejection of infant baptism then startled even those who in other respects were prepared to accept his theology."[5] The final stage came near the end of his life with the publication in 1967 of Barth's substantial volume IV/4 of his *Church Dogmatics* on baptism. Here he does two things,

     a) he confirms his rejection of infant baptism and
     b) he also rejects the term "sacrament" as properly

applicable to either baptism or the Lord's Supper and he
sees them no longer as a means of grace. He was greatly influenced by a book of his son Markus Barth entitled *Die
Taufe ein Sacrament?*[7]–Is Baptism a Sacrament? When he
examined and expounded the New Testament he was con-
vinced that it did not support a sacramental view of water
baptism. There is now for him only one *sacramentum* or
mystery, that of the incarnation, the Word in the act of reconciliation. This does not mean that baptism and the Lord's
Supper are abandoned; rather they continue to have a central and significant place as testimonies to grace given and
as affirmations and means of our response, of confessing
before God and humanity in the Christian community that
we have received the grace of our Lord Jesus Christ and are
resolved to walk in his ways. Baptism is not therefore left
to the side but has two forms. There is baptism by the Holy
Spirit which is God's act apart from what we call baptism,
and there is the purely human act of water baptism in response to God's gracious work for us in reconciliation and
in us by the Holy Spirit. Even his friends have asked: Is it
necessary to make such a wholesale separation between the
two? Could not the sign remain a means of grace and not
simply a way of man's response? Even if one abandons infant baptism, as Jürgen Moltmann does[8], does one necessarily abandon the sacramental view of baptism? T. F. Torrance[9] feels there is here the danger of a real division and
dualism in our thought and practice, and in Barth's, at this
point.
     Yet Barth's purpose is not so much to pull down as
to build up, to counter indiscriminate baptism, to state a
proper biblical doctrine and to advocate a practice in accord
with this. He realizes that his teaching at the end of his life
put him in an isolated position but states, "the day will
come when justice will be done to me in this matter too. I
hazard the paradoxical conjecture that this will perhaps
come about earlier, not on our side, but among Roman
Catholic theologians who to-day are questioning almost
everything—unless a new Pius IX blights the present hopes

of blossom."[10]

This was written in 1967 just after Vatican II, and much has happened since then. The intervening years give little ground for believing that this hope is likely to be fulfilled.

A. BAPTISM WITH THE HOLY SPIRIT

Barth teaches—and this is his main theme—that the beginning of the Christian life is God's act which brings about human faithfulness to the faithful God. This is accomplished on the basis of God's reconciliation in Christ by the power of the Holy Spirit. It is both a mystery and a miracle of grace which makes a person a new creature, a new being. In this connection he rejects three views:

a) The popular Catholic one of an infusion of supernatural grace, though Catholic theologians would not state it in this way nor does Vatican II.

b) The view that God's grace is merely a spur to human religious and moral impulses. This is found in ancient Pelagianism and neo-protestantism and is seen to-day in the existentialist view. No doubt he is speaking here against Rudolf Bultmann.

Barth has in mind also the views of Schleiermacher and others. Schleiermacher saw religion as natural to humanity, a feeling of absolute dependence, a God-consciousness supremely exemplified in Jesus of Nazareth. Hence grace was but a heightening of the religious and moral nature of humanity, not its change.

Barth saw the successors of Schleiermacher in Bultmann and the Christian existentialists.[11] The accusation he brings against Bultmann is that, on the basis of Heidegger's existentialism, he takes over a self-understanding of humanity as moving from inauthentic to authentic existence and makes this a pre-understanding which "controls his doctrine of the Christ event."[12] There is one exception, namely, that unlike Heidegger Bultmann sees the transition as an act of God. With this exception a philosophical pre-understanding prevails and means that the faith becomes humanity-centered. In this respect Bultmann is the heir of the nineteenth century.

c) The idea that humanity is justified but scarcely changed in this action. This is associated with Melanchthon and with later Lutheran orthodoxy.

Barth is at this point close to Calvin who "abandoned the thesis upheld by both Luther and Melanchthon, according to which the righteousness conferred upon us by justification is of a purely formal and imputed character."[13] Calvin, on the contrary saw justification and sanctification as a twofold grace and linked them more closely with our union with Christ.

Again, contrary to what Catholicism asserts, the action of the grace of God as Barth teaches (in accordance with his view of the New Testament) does not override or destroy human freedom, decision and human action—one might even say humanity's participation—but rather it inspires and enables it. God's power makes it possible for humanity to act and decide freely. There is, Barth says, "the fact that man . . . is enabled to *participate* not just passively but actively in God's grace as one who may and will and can be set to work too."[14] In this a person is changed from faithlessness to faithfulness. It is not as if God does everything and we do nothing, but because God has done everything for us in Christ, changed the whole relation between God and us, we can participate in this. Now this radical change—regeneration—where Christ speaks to us and comes to us is the work of the Holy Spirit. What Christ does for us (*pro nobis*) outside of us (*extra nos*), is now by the power of the Spirit effective in us (*in nobis*).

As we have already seen[15] the way in which the divine reconciliation becomes ours is by the resurrection opening up Christ's finished work and the significance of the cross and, by the Holy Spirit, applying it. These two are central themes of Barth's and the two ways in which Christ's life becomes ours. This can be summed up as "the power of their baptism with the Holy Ghost."[16] This change is to be sharply distinguished from water baptism since it is God's work alone, whereas the water baptism is a purely human act of confession and initiation. This baptism of the Holy Spirit awakens a person to be a witness to Jesus Christ and this essentially is what Barth believes a Christian is within the community of faith. He sums up the significance of this baptism by the Holy Spirit under five headings.

1) The Christian life begins as the living Lord Jesus Christ attests and imparts himself now by the Holy Spirit. This is done through human agents, ministers in the Church, but the Church does not represent Christ nor does he delegate his authority to another. Christ comes as Word and baptizes with the Holy Spirit. Here it is quite possible that Barth is speaking against the Catholic view of the representative nature of the hierarchy and priesthood. "The Church is neither author, dispenser, nor mediator of grace and its revelation."[17]

2) This is a form of God's grace addressed to a specific person; water baptism is not. This brings the totality of salvation, our response is always partial. This is effective, causative, creative action, wholly adequate grace, whereas humanity is receptive and only active as activated by the Holy Spirit.

3) As grace which liberates, it demands gratitude, obedience, faithfulness in freedom and Barth sees it as part of Christian ethics.

4) This new life is one of co-humanity in the communion of saints: "because it is baptism with the Holy Spirit, it is identical with his reception into the Church."[18] As such it involves no uniformity but a rich variety of charismata in individual endowments exercised in great flexibility and fluidity.

5) It is in one sense complete because of the completion of Christ's work but in another but a beginning, imperfect in us and pointing to the future, hastening towards a goal—eschatological .

Baptism with the Spirt is thus Barth's answer in a different context to the question as to how "man himself becomes the subject of this event,"[19] that is the Christian life. Barth does not deny an active human role but it is within the act of believing that a person is subject and not as co-operating with grace even if previously given. Barth's answer is put succinctly in these words: "The mystery and miracle of the event of which we speak consists in the fact that man himself is the free subject of this event on the basis of a possibility which is present only with God."[20] God the supreme Subject alone enables one to believe and oneself become a subject who actually does believe. Barth rightly underlines both the mystery and miracle of grace by the Spirit and the paradox of it being all of God yet also a human participatory act.

B. BAPTISM WITH WATER

We have seen that there are really two baptisms, distinct but interrelated—baptism with the Holy Spirit which makes a person new and free for faithfulness to God, and baptism by water. Looking at these two in their inter-relationship Barth writes, "Baptism with the Holy Spirit does not exclude baptism with water . . . Indeed, it makes it possible and demands it. Again, baptism with water is what it is only in relation to baptism with the Holy Spirit."[21] There would be no baptism with water at all were it not for baptism with the Holy Spirit which brings us the grace of God and enables us to believe. The human is in response and corresponds to this divine action. The divine baptism enables a person in freedom and gratitude to make a total life-act of commitment and obedience. In token of this one comes and asks for the human act of water baptism to confirm what has happened by the Spirit right at the beginning of the Christian life. Barth writes, "Christian baptism is the first form of the human decision which in the foundation of the Christian life corresponds to the divine change."[22] So the request for water baptism as a ratification of this newly-given freedom is itself a free act of the human responding to and reflecting the divine change wrought for a person by

Christ and made effective by the Holy Spirit. Thus baptism with water becomes for Barth a human confession before God and his people and not a divine action or means of grace. Again, it is an act of the Church and not of a special ministry within the Church. Here he is critical of yet also comes closer to the Catholic position. "There is in the New Testament no transfer of the *potestas* and competence to baptize to a specific circle with a particular ecclesiastical office."[23] This means that anyone can baptize though, no doubt, it would be the ordained ministers of the Church who would normally do so.

Barth goes on to outline three different aspects of water baptism;[24] (a) its basis, (b) its goal, (c) its meaning. We look at these in turn.

a) The *Basis* of Baptism.

The will and work of the Lord himself is its sure and adequate basis—but how? Is it his command as in Matthew 28:19 to go and baptize—words which may or may not be the *ipsissima verba* of Jesus? Even if they are the words of the community they clearly reflect the whole intention of Jesus' life and ministry, of his death and resurrection—to make disciples of all nations and baptize them as such.

The real basis is not so much, however, in specific words as in Jesus' action in submitting himself to John's baptism as the sin-bearer in a life which was itself moving towards the decisive baptism of his death for human sin. By this action Jesus submitted himself to the Father's will, confessed that will about to be done on earth and set himself in solidarity with sinful human beings for their salvation. In this way he took up his service as Messiah and Saviour. In doing so he pointed to his own baptism in obedience to the same will of God. Hartwell writes, that while the Holy Spirit was the act of God at Jesus' baptism confirming it "Jesus' water-baptism was a human work, a humble act of obedience."[25]

It is also, therefore, in the light of Jesus' own baptism that Matthew 28:19 is to be understood, namely, as the realization after the completion of his own saving work and baptism of the will of the Lord for his people.

b) The *Goal* of Baptism.

The basis is at the same time the goal, namely, Jesus Christ himself in his work of reconciliation already accomplished. Nevertheless there is a future aspect to it. By the Holy Spirit this reconciliation is to be received not just once but repeatedly by us. We look forward and move towards this goal. The goal is not in itself, in that act, nor is it in the faith of the community or the candidate for baptism. The act itself has no inherent efficacy either in the individual or in the rite but it is a joint confession of faith by the community and the individual of the Lordship of the reconciling Christ.

Water baptism is thus a confession that the faith and new life we have received are divine acts and gifts to us. Baptism is thus not a means of grace, as we have seen, but an acknowledgment of grace and a pointer to further grace. It is in no way a second salvation event. Here Barth is probably speaking against the views of Oscar Cullman, Catholics and others.[26] Nor is it an instrument or channel of grace. Christ is not the subject of baptism. One could sum up by saying that it is a movement towards the Christ who has reconciled (christological). It has him as the end or goal (eschatological) and as the practical purpose our participation in the life of Christ through faith within the Christian community (teleological).[27]

c) The *Meaning* of Baptism.

As we have already seen, for Barth water baptism is essentially a human response to the divine grace, corresponding to it, correlated with it, answering it. Here we have a very special emphasis throughout the *Church Dogmatics* (particularly the later parts) that what we do is always a testimony. There are therefore two aspects of the meaning of Baptism.

Negatively, it is not a supposedly immanent divine work, i.e., not a sacrament in any usual sense of the term, "not itself . . . the bearer, means, or instrument of grace."[28]

This is a critique of Catholic, Lutheran and Reformed Church views. To make it such would be to destroy "man's free, responsible response in baptism to God's work in Jesus Christ."[29] The divine would overwhelm and submerge the human. Here one may remark that it is somewhat ironic that Barth, who has been repeatedly criticised on all sides for undervaluing the human, now turns the tables on his critics, or, at any rate accuses others of precisely this error.

To be sure God is active here in evoking human response but not in using baptism as a sacrament. And it is not a sacrament for this reason: a sacrament or mystery refers exclusively to God's action in Christ and not to our response and faith. In an extensive exposition of the biblical passages Barth comes to the conclusion that they are not necessarily sacramental, though he is also cautious on this issue.[31]

Positively, Barth characterizes this step as a form of turning, repentance, conversion, "leaving an old path and entering upon a new."[32] There has to be a resolve, decision, act based on God's work in Christ. Here the emphasis is on human decision and not on God's grace, and more perhaps than at any other time towards the end of his life Barth emphasized the place and necessity of the human action, human response and human person. This is also a public act of the community and in the community. It is not only a turning of the person to God in and through the community, but a turning of the community with the person concerned to God. It is becoming a disciple of Jesus Christ and taking an irrevocable step. This step involves three things— obedience, renunciation of the old, and the pledge for the future to look continually to Jesus, the author and finisher of our faith.

Baptism is not absolutely necessary, according to Barth, and the exceptional circumstances—the sequence of obedience, faith, baptism which we find in the New Testament may be altered.

C. INFANT BAPTISM

Barth, quoting von Balthasar, a Catholic scholar, describes infant baptism and the decision to undertake it as "the most momentous of all decisions in Church history."[33] Up to the fourth century there was scarcely any infant baptism at all and mainly adult baptism, and neither the New Testament practice nor the doctrine of baptism itself can support infant baptism. Baptism is always related to faith and responsible decision—both quite impossible in infants; nor can the faith of others, a so-called vicarious faith do—faith, for example, of parents. Barth "asks pungently: if the candidate for baptism does not himself believe, how can his baptism be the beginning of his Christian life?" [34] The place Jesus gave to children or the covenant of grace which is said to include them is in no way a proof of its right or necessity, nor can circumcision really be said to be the forerunner of baptism in the Old Testament or a parallel to it. Thus on the basis both of early practice and of proper Christian doctrine, Barth believes that he must reject infant baptism and that the Church would be all the better if it did the same. At any rate it must look seriously at its present doctrine and pratice. Yet despite all this, Barth still regards infant baptism as not orderly but nonetheless as valid.

H. Hartwell[35] puts certain critical questions to Barth and his general position.

a) Is the division between baptism with the Holy Spirit and that of water baptism as exclusive as Barth makes it? There would seem to be doubt about this in the New Testament.

b) Is the faith by which man believes and asks for baptism not a work of the Spirit?

c) If so, can God not and does not God work through sacramental means?

d) Is water baptism a purely human work, since the Christian community prays for the coming of the Holy Spirit?

e) Is there not a subjective side to the Holy Spirit's

baptism just as there is an objective side to water baptism, so that the two are not as exclusive as Barth states?

f) Does water baptism focus simply on the baptised, so as to make infant baptism impossible? Is not grace active here also and can one divorce the two, grace and faith in the way that Barth does?

These are indeed serious questions put to Barth; no doubt he could have given a fairly adequate answer. As Hartwell shows, the importance of what he has done is that his position "represents a serious challenge to the traditional teaching on baptism and calls for a radical re-appraisal of the latter."[36]

D. EVALUATION

Karl Barth has correctly seen the position he occupies in his teaching on baptism as almost completely isolated.[37] His views are contrary to his own Reformation tradition and are closer to those of the Baptists.[38] Yet he differs considerably from these as well, and is far removed from Catholic doctrine. A brief résumé indicates the following:

a) Baptism—not a sacrament? This would seem at first sight to be consistent with Barth's christological concentration which puts Christ as the sacrament at the center and excludes all others. However, as his friends pointed out to him,[39] his view would exclude the Word (Scripture) as an instrument of the grace of God were his rejection of a sacrament to be carried to its logical conclusion.

The context and theological significance of Barth's position is important. His christological concentration means that he saw Christ as the one real sacrament and all else as testimony to this one central event. Baptism and the Lord's Supper are thus human witnesses to or signs of this one sacrament and can no longer be called sacraments. . . Barth's desacramentalising is "the necessary consequence of (his) christology."[40] Since it is Christ alone by the Holy Spirit who regenerates no positive efficacy can be ascribed to baptism or the Lord's Supper. They attest and confirm grace but do not convey it. Just as preaching does not

grace but do not convey it. Just as preaching does not create, repeat or advance the work of God but corresponds to it, reflects it, is its echo, so with baptism and the Lord's Supper.

Positively, Barth is affirming the sole efficacy of grace, and negatively, he is concerned to avoid and reject "any notion of sacrament which could be interpreted as producing in the Christian a competitive duplication of the history of Jesus Christ."[41] This danger is particularly obvious in Roman Catholicism but is implicit in Reformation positions as well. This is in accord with Barth's later teaching that preaching and the "sacraments" so-called are significative. They point to, bear witness to Christ, but are not instrumental to saving effect. This latter point can be granted. Again it can be granted that there are certain ways the witnesses should not be understood, namely, as automatically effective, or as rivalling Christ, or as second salvation events.

But Gollwitzer's question must still be pressed: must a "sign" and an "instrument" be set against one another? It is scarcely necessary, even on Barth's own premises, to make such a total separation. If one comes to baptism already believing is not Hartwell's statement true that in the human response and request for, as in the act of baptism itself, the Holy Spirit is also operative? In this sense a certain "sacramental" view of the sign in inevitable and possible though perhaps with less emphasis than heretofore. Does opposition to and almost automatic sacramentalism exclude all human and natural instrumental action? Barth in fact answers the objection by saying that the Church is always in danger of exalting the means and misusing them, but he does not deny that God by the Spirit uses means ever and again.

The main point that he is making is the important one that the work of grace is God's work alone by the Holy Spirit, that witnesses are signs pointing to this but not instruments that contribute to it in any way. This need not necessarily, indeed cannot, exclude their use by God himself to come, speak and act by the Holy Spirit. This distinc-

ment" or "means" of grace could be largely a verbal one.

In this case Barth could perhaps have accepted with some reserve a sacramental view of the "'signs".

Eberhard Busch has put Barth's position clearly[42] when he quotes the *Church Dogmatics*, "human beings know God in that they stand before God,"[43] and comments: "If read carefully and interpreted correctly, it sounds a whole range of positive theses and negative antitheses characteristic of Barth."[44] God is different from us, over against us, beyond our power of disposal but known as he turns to us and gives himself to be known in Jesus Christ by the Holy Spirit.

"Something else one can hear from that sentence, something which from his middle period onward Barth impressed upon himself more and more rigorously: the critique of the conception of preaching which saw preaching as having a mediating-instrumental function. He extended that critique to similar conceptions of the sacraments, of any activity of the Church, of Christianity and theology, yes, to any such conceptions of the Church itself. This critique seeks decisively to prevent people from departing from that situation of being before God in their activities and existence which such a conception would cause. They depart from it and cast it behind their backs in the belief of standing on God's side, of having the divine at their disposition and being able to mediate, apply or transform it. For Barth, on the other hand, the Holy Spirit alone is *mediator* of salvation in the actual sense of that term. Human beings, meanwhile, in all their ecclesial, Christian and theological activities can always only *remain* standing in that situation of being before God. Therefore, in all those activities and, hence, in continuous solidarity with other human beings, that is, without ever being able to leave it behind, they can be only witnesses, in the strictest sense of the word. The sentence, that human beings know God in that they stand before God, contains *in nuce* an entire theology."[45]

b) The second issue in Barth's baptismal views is his biblical exposition. His exegesis is a possible though unusual one and not to be dismissed out of hand. He believes many of the passages usually adduced as relating to water-Baptism refer to the Spirit primarily or alone. His view[46] (following Calvin) on, for example, John 3:5 that water is simply a repetition of Spirit, is not entirely convincing. In other words one cannot conclusively accept his exposition as the basis for his deductions. His own conclusions admit this explicitly.[47]

c) His views diverge from both Lutheran and Reformed teaching which regards baptism and the Lord's Supper as sacraments and accepts infant baptism. Yet Barth's views are a real challenge to these traditions to re-think their positions in the light of his questioning and his exposition of Scripture. At the same time Barth would not accept readily the Baptist view which he would probably regard as much too subjective, placing too much emphasis on human decision as well as on the work of the Holy Spirit.

d) Neither Barth nor the Churches of the Reformation tradition can accept the Catholic position which states[48] at Vatican II that baptism works *ex opere operato* given a proper and not a negative disposition, and that it as such regenerates. Nor could they agree that it is the foundation which makes it possible for man to meet God in the future i.e., to enter fully into the sacramental life of the Catholic Church. All this, says Vatican II,[49] flows from baptism and leads to Catholicism. While baptism marks the entry into the Church it does not work *ex opere operato* nor is it absolutely essential to salvation. Barth very clearly points us to the work of the Spirit and the need for personal profession of faith. If this does not necessarily deny, it at least queries both infant baptism and the teaching that in baptism we are all brought into the Body of Christ.

Perhaps the most telling point to be made here is that in both Catholic and Protestant views on infant baptism the person concerned most directly is entirely passive. Karl Barth has emphasized most strongly what Catholics in particular persistently accuse him of i.e., not giving a place and active participation to humanity. Is this not nearer the

New Testament witness and does it not point to a serious weakness in the Catholic and other traditions to which much more attention should be given?

One of the most thorough examinations and critiques of Barth's teaching on baptism has been made by E. Jüngel.[50] Among many points he makes the following. Barth's baptismal teaching is to be understood in the context of his theology as a whole and particularly in the light of his doctrine of reconciliation. Barth sees Jesus as representative man and thus as the one sacrament of divine grace. This in turn corrects and excludes the traditional Reformation view of baptism as a sacrament and as a means of grace. At the same time it affirms the true Reformation insight of salvation as God's act alone by the Holy Spirit. Water baptism thus becomes an analogy (*analogatum*), a self-affirmation, of what one is in Christ (*analogans*), but is not a means of grace.

Moreover, since water-baptism is a human answer to grace it involves conscious participation and so excludes the possibility of infant baptism. But because it is a human act in response to grace already given by the Holy Spirit, it makes possible a double ecumenical dialogue, namely, with Baptists on the one hand and with Roman Catholics on the other.

Jüngel sees this position as basically correct but believes Barth has not fully clarified several issues. He mentions three in particular: the variety of baptismal understanding to be found within the New Testament; the relationship between baptism and sin; and the difficulties of making a clear distinction between Spirit-baptism and water-baptism. Nevertheless, Jüngel regards Barth's denial of the sacramental nature of baptism as consistent with his christological concentration so that if one cannot follow Barth here one will find problems with his earlier work.

NOTES

1. John Calvin, *The Institutes of the Christian Religion*, Ed. John T. McNeill, trs. Ford Lewis Battles, London: S.C.M. 1961, IV, XIV, 1.

2. Karl Barth, *The Epistle to the Romans*, trs. Edwyn C. Hoskyns, Oxford University Press, 6th Edition 1968, p. 192; cf. also *The Holy Ghost and the Christian Life*, trs. R. Birch Hoyle, London; F. Muller, 1938, p. 84; *C.D.*, 1/1, p. 154; *Ethics*, trs. G. W. Bromiley of Barth's *Ethik*, 1928, Edinburgh: T.& T. Clark, 1981, pp. 105-106.

3. Karl Barth, *The Teaching of the Church regarding Baptism*, trs. E. A. Payne, London, S.C.M. 1948. But see Eberhard Busch, *Karl Barth, His life from letters and biographical texts*, trs. John Bowden, London: S.C.M. 1976[2] where in 1938 Barth writes in a letter to A. Koechlin that he "came to completely negative conclusions over Calvin's argument for infant baptism." Ibid., p. 286.

4. H. Hartwell, "Karl Barth on Baptism," *SJT* XXII 1969, p. 12.

5. Ibid., pp. 12-13.

6. Karl Barth, *C.D.*, IV/4, "Fragment, Baptism as the Foundation of the Christian Life," Edinburgh: T & T Clark, 1969.

7. Ibid., p. x.

8. Jürgen Moltmann, *The Church in the Power of the Spirit*, trs. Margaret Kohl, London: S.C.M., 1978[2], pp. 226 ff.

9. T. F. Torrance, *Theology in Reconciliation*, London: Geoffrey Chapman, 1975, p. 99.

10. *C.D.*, IV/4 p. xii.

11. Karl Barth, "Rudolf Bultmann—An Attempt to Understand Him," *Kerygma and Myth*, II, p. 114.

12. Ibid.

13. François Wendel, *Calvin*, trs. Philip Mairet, Collins: Fontana Library, 1976, p. 236.

14. *C.D.*, IV/4, p. 6; Italics mine.

15. See above chapter V.

16. *C.D.*, IV/4, p. 30.

17. Ibid., p. 32.

18. Ibid., p. 37.

19. Ibid., p. 4.

20. Ibid., p. 5.

21. Ibid., p. 41.

22. Ibid., p. 44.

23. Ibid., p. 49. He believes that no priestly office is necessary for baptism (so *contra* Catholicism) but sees it as an act of the Church, thus coming nearer the Catholic view that any lay person can baptize in an emergency.

24. Ibid., pp. 50 ff.

25. Op.cit., p. 21.

26. *C.D.*, IV/4, p. 88. "Where did we find even a hint that in, with and under the water baptism administered and received by men there takes place a continuation, repetition or doublet of the divine act of salvation and revelation." Cf. Oscar Cullmann, *Baptism in the New Testament*, trs. J. K. S. Reid, London: S.C.M., 1950, p. 35, where Cullmann tries to refute this accusation, namely, that his views scarcely differ from Catholics, Anglicans and Lutherans.

27. Ibid., p. 89.

28. Ibid., p. 102.

29. Hartwell, op.cit., p. 23.

30. *C.D.*, IV/4, pp. 111-127.

31. Ibid., p. 128, where Barth speaks of his findings as "probable" but open to better instruction.

32. Ibid., p. 135.

33. See *C.D.*, IV/4, p. 164.

34. Hartwell, op.cit., pp. 26-27.

35. Ibid., pp. 28-29.

36. Ibid., p. 29.

37. C.D., IV/4., p. xii, "I forsee that this book . . . will leave me in the theological and ecclesiastical isolation which has been my lot for almost fifty years."

38. Ibid., p. 193.

39. Klappert, *Promissio und Bund*, pp. 273-274. These discussions took place with Professsors H. Gollwitzer and H. Diem.

40. Ibid., p. 163, n. 1.

41. Rosato, op.cit., p. 114.

42. Eberhard Busch, Introduction in *Karl Barth in Re-View Posthumous Works Reviewed and Assessed*, ed. H.-Martin Rumscheidt,

Pittsburgh: The Pickwick Press, 1981, p. xv.
    43. *C.D.*, II/1, p. 9.
    44. Busch. op.cit., p. xv.
    45. Ibid., p. xvi.
    46. *C D.*, IV/4, pp. 120-121.
    47. See note 31 above.
    48. Ibid, p. 363.
    49. Walter M. Abbott, ed. *Documents of Vatican II*, Decree on
Ecumenism, London: Geoffrey Chapman, 1967, Ibid., pp. 363-364.
    50. E. Jüngel, *Barth-Studien*, Gütersloher Verlagshaus, Gerd
Mohn, Benzinger Verlag, 1982, pp. 246ff.

CHAPTER EIGHT

THE HOLY SPIRIT AND THE INDIVIDUAL

We have seen that Karl Barth sets his doctrine of the Church in the context of his doctrine of reconciliation and as this latter is viewed in three perspectives, so also is the Church. The same holds good for the individual Christian within the community, and it is always as an individual within the community that Barth thinks of the Christian. The Christian life is seen as a life called forth and sustained by the Holy Spirit, and as having three aspects corresponding to (a) the calling and gathering, (b) the upbuilding and (c) the sending of the community. These three aspects are faith, love and hope and to these we now come in turn.

A. FAITH

A characteristic and comprehensive way in which Barth sees faith is summed up in a short passage on the knowledge of God.[1] Faith is from first to last the work of the Holy Spirit. In this passage the trinitarian basis is again in evidence: "The life of the Church and the life of the children of God is, as the work of the Holy Spirit, nothing but the unity of the Father and the Son in the form of time, among and in us men whose existence as such is not yet at home with the Lord but still in the far country, although in Jesus Christ it is no longer in the far country but already at home with the Lord."[2] By this Barth means that we are already with Christ and at the Father's side through reconciliation but not yet there because we live in space and time. Since we know the gift of faith by the Holy Spirit our life has an eschatological existence, already with the Lord in a pure present but not yet with him in the ultimate consummation. This life in the Spirit is the life of faith not sight. Faith has therefore this present and yet future dimension. It is not something merely inward or immanent; it is a new birth and life from above: "As the work of the Holy Spirit it is man's new birth from God, on the basis of which man can already live here by what he is there in Jesus Christ and therefore in truth. Faith is the temporal form of his eternal being in Jesus Christ, his being which is grounded on the fact that Jesus Christ intercedes for us before the Father."[3] Our reality as human beings is objectively included in Jesus Christ "there and then" in reconciliation, and so in the triune life of God. In one sense we are already within; but not until we receive the gift of the Spirit and so have faith is this truth actually ours. We possess the knowledge of God or are possessed by it in faith and so also in promise and hope. It is not merely promise but both present and to come.

In this present perspective trinitarian, christological, eschatological and pneumatic aspects are all interrelated to give us the one comprehensive truth of the triune God active in Christ by the Holy Spirit who creates faith in us. Here again we see Barth's theological ontology.

Barth thus sees faith as the work of God and particularly that of the Holy Spirit. He writes, "The Holy Spirit is the awakening power in which Jesus Christ summons a sinful man to his community and therefore as a Christian to believe in him; to acknowledge and know and confess him as the Lord who for him became a servant."[4] Barth therefore makes faith and the believing person the end point of his whole doctrine in contrast to the nineteenth century theologians and to Schleiermacher in particular, who made it central, and a fact that was generally known. Similar views, though in a different context, have been expressed by pietism, the evangelical wing of the continental Protestant Churches and by modern existentialism, which centers on the individual and personal experience and gives minimal emphasis to the Church. For Barth, however, faith is real-

ized within the context of the believing community. Faith
belongs to the third article of the Creed, but must be seen
also in relation to Jesus Christ who is both its object and its
source. Faith is thus a human activity (in one sense) though
orientated to and coming from Christ by the Holy Spirit,
but is never a human possibility. It is never something that
we can summon up on our own. It is true of course that a
person must choose and does choose what Barth would say
is the only real course open to us that is, to believe. Its opposite is an absurd—unreal course determined for destruc-
tion and death; here we come up against Barth's view of
evil as something which is actual but has no true reality,
does not belong to that realm which endures. It is here that
we meet with an aspect of Barth's ontology. Humanity is
realiter not godless but has an ontological connection with
God by God's act in binding himself to it in the incarnation.
Unbelief is thus an ontological impossibility. But it is in
fact there and actual since humanity by its sin contradicts
its real being in Christ. Unbelief is an "impossible possibility" (eine unmögliche Möglichkeit). The only *real* alternative for humanity is faith; unbelief is unfreedom and slavery, a terrible *actuality* but ontologically unreal. The Holy
Spirit alone in the freedom and grace of God can release us
from the impossible servitude of sin to the reality of our being in faith. Barth writes, "The Holy Spirit is the power in
which Jesus Christ, the Son of God, makes a man free,
makes him genuinely free for this choice and therefore for
faith."[5]
          Moreover in this a person takes on a new form of
existence, the reality of humanity made new, yet acting as
subject with free choice and responsibility. Here our active
willing as subject and free response are clearly affirmed
and underlined. It is quite wrong to think that Barth's view
is "God is everything and humanity is nothing;" it is in fact
in and through God acting by the Holy Spirit that a person
comes to faith and in this act of believing expresses his true
existence and real humanity. Otherwise expressed, God
acts always as the God of humanity and for us in Christ by
the Holy Spirit; and because this is so, a person who be-

lieves and who now exists in faith, is a new being, a new creation, has a new birth from above. Further, as such the individual is like the community, there not simply for itself or alone or isolated. The individual is the representative of the whole of humanity to which God has addressed himself in Jesus Christ and which he has reconciled in him; in this way the believer is a forerunner of what is the will of God for humanity as a whole..

Barth fully recognises and affirms that it is the Christian community that is awakened to faith but adds that while this is true "the creaturely subject awakened as such by the power of the Holy Spirit is in the last resort the individual Christian in the act of his personal faith."[6] The two are in fact one. In and through the calling of the community the individual is called to personal faith in Jesus Christ and obedience to him. Thus Jesus Christ, the Son, humbled to death and bearing our sins in atonement, includes not only the world and all humanity, not only his own, the Christian community, but also me. He is *pro me* (for me) as well as *pro nobis* (for us) and *propter nos homines* (for us human beings). It is precisely for me that Christ came and died and his work has reached me by the Holy Spirit: "God did not will to be God without being just his God. Jesus did not will to be Jesus without being just his Jesus."[7] Yet this faith must be set in the wider context of what Christ is and has done both for the Church and for the world. This individualistic emphasis, so far as it goes, is right in Luther, in pietism, in Kierkegaard, in Herrmann and existentialism, but it is wrong and becomes false and dangerous when made central and isolated from its context in the Church and in the objective reconciliation of the world in Jesus Christ. Here is a place where Barth partially agrees with but also differs from Rudolf Bultmann and where he believes the latter goes astray in making the center what is "existentially" relevant to the individual. Bultmann's theory is much too individualistic.

According to Barth the act of faith has itself three aspects. Traditional post-Reformation Protestantism spoke of it as *notitia, assensus, fiducia* (knowledge, assent and faith or trust). These aspects are and must be there, but, Barth believes, in a different order and with a somewhat different emphasis. He speaks, therefore, of them as acknowledgment (*anerkennen*), knowledge (*erkennen*), confession (*bekennen*).[8] All, be it noted, are forms of knowledge; this does not mean that faith is simply intellectual, but nonetheless each way of believing contains a knowledge of God and brings us a true understanding of who he is in Jesus Christ by the Holy Spirit.

a) Faith is acknowledgment of Jesus Christ himself as Lord, as my Lord and my God, as Thomas has it. Here again, Herrmann and Bultmann are right as far as they go. Faith is not first of all doctrine but life, not theory but a personal, practical relationship to Jesus Christ. Barth is very fond of quoting Calvin at this point, who said that all knowledge begins in obedience.[9]

b) Faith is at the same time true knowledge of God in Jesus Christ and what he has done for us. But it is never a knowledge abstracted from the act of faith, of believing nor without real content. The reality of faith is itself throughout a form of knowledge. Moreover this knowledge of Christ includes a knowledge about the believing person in accordance with the Scriptures. It is not *fides implicita*, (implicit faith) as Catholicism puts it, an implicit believing in what is handed down, nor on the other hand, does the believing subject in any way repeat or represent the existence and reality of Jesus Christ in his being and work for us. Here Barth is speaking against Bultmann's existentialism and against Roman Catholic doctrine and sacramental teaching as represented by von Balthasar. There is analogy, correspondence and response but there is no second salvation event rivaling that of Jesus Christ:[10]

"Barth will not compromise with any attempt—whether Roman Catholic, Reformational, Neo-Protestant or Existential—to confuse Christ and the Christian. There can be no representation or re-enactment of Christ's life in that of the Christian. There can only be a pneumatological synthesis of the two independent realities once the Holy Spirit has created a reflection of Christ's being in the being of the community."[11]

    c) Faith is also confession.[12] A Christian is one who testifies to personal faith, is a witness to Jesus Christ and of the glory of God manifest in him. Faith takes cognisance of what has been given and itself is a form of giving. As a little light the Christian bears witness to the great light. This is required of a believer not only by the object of faith but by the nature of the fellowship which exists for the world that is in ignorance and does not know. So a Christian is one who stands for Christ and bears witness to him both by words and works.

    In one sense when we speak of faith we must speak of it as cognitive. It is simply acknowledging, knowing, and testifying to what God has done in Jesus Christ and which we could not in any sense do for ourselves. But, at the same time, faith is a human activity awakened and created in us contrary to our sinful nature and will by the power of the Holy Spirit. In this way a person becomes a new subject, a new creation by a new birth so that one's faith is not merely passive but active, "not merely cognitive as a human act but it is also creative in character" as the work of the Holy Spirit.

B. LOVE

    It is again the Holy Spirit who is the quickening power by which Jesus Christ gives humanity freedom to love. It is a freedom to be active in self-giving love to God and one's fellows, that draws us up to God and enables us to overcome our sloth and misery; here the second aspect of the doctrine of Christ comes in—humanity which is exalted. Faith and love stand in the same relationship to each other as do justification and sanctification. They are twin aspects of the one movement of grace in humanity, just as justification and sanctification are twin aspects of the one movement of God to humanity and also for us. Love is involved in and follows faith as sanctification follows justification. It is both there in faith and as the outworking of faith in discipleship, in subordination to Christ as the exalted King. It is the true and royal way.

But what is love? It is an act of self-giving in response to God's action for us in Jesus Christ: "Love as self-giving stands contrasted with faith as reception."[14] Faith works by love (Gal 5:6). It is faith in action and not an activity "which is added as a second thing making it a *fides formata* (formed faith) as the later expression had it."[15] This is spoken against the Roman Catholic view of a *fides caritate formata* (faith formed by love). In the Roman Catholic view faith justifies because it is "penetrated with our love of God and man."[16] In the view of the Reformers and Barth "faith is penetrated with love because it 'justifies'."[17] It is *"fides a Christo formata,* (faith formed by Christ) and, since Christ is its *forma,* it produces love and works by it."[18] What is being said here is that in the view of Barth and the Reformers faith and love are formed at the same time by Christ. While the Roman Catholic view does not deny this, it puts the emphasis on a love coming from Christ which forms faith; a person is not justified until this faith is formed by love By contrast, in the Reformed view it is through our faith that we are justified by the grace of God; one does not have to wait until faith has been formed by love for such justification to take place.

Love is therefore the Christian activity par excellence, the more excellent way. The Greek term is *Agape,* self-giving love, based on the self-giving love of God in Christ. This love turns to the other for its own sake, demanding nothing from the other, making no claims upon another. It is specifically in this royal freedom that it is distinguished from *eros* (human love)—an idea which the New Testament, Barth notes, does not have at all. In contrasting *agape* and *eros,* he refers sometimes approvingly, sometimes critically, to the well-known book of Anders Nygren, *Agape and Eros.*[19] *Agape* gives itself, *Eros* is a form of selfassertion, demanding, wanting. They are basically moving in opposite directions. The one is self-love, the other selfgiving. The latter is only possible by the quickening and enabling power of the Holy Spirit; it is the love absolutely superior to eros not only in dignity but also in power, overcoming it and in fact replacing it.

Barth speaks of three ways in which this love may be viewed, first of all, the basis of love in the triune God, secondly, the act of love in our human being and existence, and thirdly, the object of love towards which it is directed.

a) The basis of Love

In a way quite typical of his whole theology and its nature Barth points to the basis of love in the triune God himself who is a love which is free, eloquent and dynamic. We have noted already[20] that the Trinity stands at the very beginning of Barth's whole doctrine, and that the nature of the triune God determines the whole of the nature of his theology; here again, at this particular point, we see this coming to the fore. What Barth is saying is as follows: The Holy Spirit is, in his view (following Augustine), the bond of love of the Father and the Son and so a mutual and eternal self-giving union and love. Yet it is its very nature as this kind of eternal love that makes it possible in free grace to reach out and overflow to us from all eternity, embracing us, including us and in time redeeming us in love and by the Holy Spirit enabling us to love. Thus, in Barth's view, God moves within himself as the one who loves in freedom and moves out to us by the same Holy Spirit. In the New Testament the love of God is seen in Jesus Christ and comes by the Holy Spirit: "The love of God is the creative work of the Holy Spirit. As God is Spirit, the Spirit of the Father and the Son, as he gives himself into human life as Spirit, and as he bears witness as Spirit to our spirit that we are his children (Rom 8:16), God gives us to participate in the love in which as Father he loves the Son and as Son the Father, making our action a reflection of his eternal love and ourselves those who may and will love."[21] Otto Weber puts it in this way, "As love God reaches out of himself by the Holy Spirit, makes us free by the power of his love and enables us to imitate God himself."[22] Christian love is thus nothing less than the love of the triune God active and reflected in us by the Holy Spirit.

b) The Act of Love

Here we turn from the basis to think of what is the nature of that divine love expressed in human life. In so far as one is a Christian one loves and this love has the character of a free, spontaneous act because this freedom and character are given to a person by God. It shows itself as something new, unusual and unexpected. In this it is again contrasted with eros which is always natural and quite predictable. Barth writes, "If it takes place at all, it does so in a mighty act of the Holy Ghost for whom we can only pray, whose presence and action can only cause grateful astonishment even to those who are active in love, let alone to others."[23]

Again, it is the free act of a human being and not simply a prolongation of the divine love. Here we have the paradox which is at the heart of our faith, that it is both God's work by the Spirit and it is also ours in a human act of believing. Barth underlines this again when he states, "it is not the work of the Holy Spirit to take from man his own proper activity, or to make it simply a function of his own overpowering control . . . but the work of the Holy Spirit consists in the liberation of man for his own act and therefore for the spontaneous human love whose littleness and frailty are his own responsibility and not that of the Holy Spirit."[24] Here is Barth's answer to those Roman Catholic critics who would say that he is giving no proper place to human response and that humanity is overshadowed and takes no share in this work. Humanity in fact is given by the Holy Spirit the freedom to be itself, itself to act in believing and in loving.

Nor can or should we think and speak of this love as simply a disposition or thought, emotion or feeling; it is an act corresponding to God's redeeming act in Jesus Christ. If love is the outworking of faith it is a work, not a work that is meritorious in the sense of deserving salvation, but a work which is seen in self-giving. It is also seen as humanity being exalted, as a form of gain and joy, a joy not simply of others' response to one's love or of one's own self-satisfaction, but a joy which is inherent in the very nature

of loving, because it reflects and comes from the divine nature as love itself.[25]

c) The Object of Love

This can quite simply be summed up in the phrase
of Jesus, love God and love your neighbour. While the two
are interrelated and are in a sense one, it would be quite
wrong and misleading to fail to see and underline the order
and priority here, for love to God determines the nature of
one's love for one's neighbour and therefore it must come
first.

1) *Love to God.* This is not simply equivalent to
love for one's neighbour; they are inseparable but not to be
identified. This is against the idea of Albrecht Ritschl[26] and
of writers like John Robinson[27] who felt that it is in commitment to human love that the divine reality itself is
reached. Rather, as we have seen, since God loves us we
may quite simply love God and do so in the freedom and
power of the Holy Spirit, obeying God willingly and not by
constraint. The freedom for love means freedom to obey,
freedom to act according to the will of God to whom we all
belong.

Barth, therefore, takes up the question of the relationship of love to freedom and obedience; this reflects a
further basic interest in his whole theology. When he
speaks of the attributes of God, he puts them under two aspects of the divine nature, the love and the freedom of
God.[28] God is one who loves in freedom and who is free in
his love, and this is reflected in human life because we become the children of God which means freedom to call God
our Father and freedom to obey him. Obedience, therefore,
according to Barth, is not simply something that we do because God has commanded us to do it, though it has that
element in it as well. Rather is it something we do because
God has liberated us by his creative love and awakened us
by the power of the Holy Spirit. In this way, therefore, he
has so bound us to himself that we give him a willing and a
free obedience. Love is therefore of grace, of the Spirit and
not merely of law. Yet, says Barth, "obedience is the re-
quired action of love, i.e., the action of love which is de-

manded by love itself . . . to be quickened by the Holy Spirit is to move oneself, and to do so in obedience, listening to the order and command of God."[29] Again, Barth draws attention to two important aspects of all this. It is not God alone who acts in this but a human person acts in love and in obedience even though this is done by the power and inspiration of the Holy Spirit. Further, a person acts in obedience to the living God: obedience is no static quality but a living, dynamic one. By this Barth means that it takes place in our continual meeting with him who is the living, acting, loving God. In this "man is constantly referred to God's own presence and encounter with him, to the eternal love which is the basis of his love, to the work and gift of the Holy Spirit."[30]

Barth sees the divine freedom and love by the power of the Spirit as the basis of ethics—a theological ethics. Within the Spirit's action is the power to love in obedience and conform to God's way and will and law.

2) *Love to neighbour*. The object of one's love is not only God, but also human beings. Almost surprisingly Barth states that "it may sound harsh at first, but we have to note that neither the Old Testament nor the New speaks of a love for man as such and therefore for all men; of a universal love of humanity."[31] Rather the neighbour is one called and chosen, set in a very definite relationship to us, namely, in Israel and the Church, so that here we are talking in the context of the history of salvation. We live to some extent in a closed circle and the only exception that is mentioned in the New Testament is I Thess 3:12, and also the command to love one's enemy. To love one's neighbour is to love one's fellow-Christian, one's brother and sister in Christ. To live in love in community is not an end in itself. To love one's neighbour may not be equal to a universal love for humanity, but does not exclude it, since the community is but the provisional and practical form of what we are all meant to be. Otto Weber sums up Barth's position in this way, "The believer must keep an openness for ever new meetings and demands."[32] Barth himself writes, "Those who themselves exist in this context of the history

of salvation, and may therefore love God and their neigh-
bours, have no option in this respect. They must be ready
and on the way to love for all, even in relationships in
which its realization is at the moment impossible . . . It certainly must be said that, while the circle of vital Christian
love for the neighbour is not the sphere of all men indis-
criminately, it is not a hermetically sealed circle within this
sphere, but one which continually broadens out into it."[33]
        To love is not, therefore, an operation in self-help.
We cannot do this of ourselves. We are inspired and enabled by the Holy Spirit. Barth states, "This kind of exertion
is quite futile, since none can do it. Only by the Holy Spirit
do they become free for this action. But by the Holy Spirit
they do become free for it. By the Holy Spirit the individual
becomes free for existence in an active relationship with
the other in which he is loved and finds that he may love in
return."[34]
        In Barth's theology faith is co-ordinated with justifi-
cation and love with sanctification. Both are realities in Jesus Christ who is himself our justification and sanctification (objectively). Yet these two become ours through faith,
through our union with Christ by the Holy Spirit. Barth follows Calvin closely here in seeing them as a twofold grace
(*duplex gratia*)—one yet distinct. The ultimate goal of
God's action for us and in us is sanctification but the order
within the one divine action is justification and sanctification. By the Holy Spirit we are brought to faith, set right
with God, justified, forgiven and, in one and the same act,
set in a process which makes us holy. What sanctifies us is
participation in Christ, the Holy One. A person, while re-
maining a sinner, becomes a "saint", is a "disturbed sinner",
one whose sin no longer is allowed to rule, one in whom "a
real change"[35] is wrought, "a real alteration of their being."[36] A limitation is set to their sin; they are lifted up in a
new direction and given the sovereignty, power and freedom of the Spirit. United with Christ by the same Holy
Spirit the Christian life reflects, corresponds to the exalted
life of Christ at the right hand of the Father. It is to this
Christ—who by the Holy Spirit creates new life in us—that

the "Holy Ones" are called to bear witness.

The Holy Spirit is therefore not only the power of Christ drawing us to himself in faith, but keeping us with him in love and giving us the grace of his holiness in constant conflict with, and opposition to, our sin.

C. HOPE

Just as faith is related to the calling and gathering of the community and love to its upbuilding, so hope concerns its sending and mission "to the ends of the earth" and "to the end of time" (to use phrases popularised by J. Lesslie Newbigin in his book, *The Household of God*).[38] We are here in the region of eschatology and since another chapter deals with this, the question is touched on only very briefly. For Barth hope is faith directed to the end, to the final revelation and consummation, and is based on all God has already done in Jesus Christ, especially in his death and resurrection. It is hope in God himself and so is a sure and certain hope: "We can and should say that the Christian believes in the One who came then, that he loves him as the One who is present now and that he hopes for his new coming one day."[39] Here Barth shows both the interrelationship of faith, love and hope and that each has the same Subject as its object, namely, Jesus Christ himself—the One in whom we believe, the One whom we love and the One for whose coming we hope at the last day. While each has the one object it has a distinctive time and orientation.

This hope is not merely for the individual but for the consummation of the whole created cosmos: "In hoping in Jesus Christ, the Christian hopes for the glory of God investing the whole creation of God of every time and place with unspotted and imperishable glory."[40] The Spirit is the pledge and foretaste of this future redemption at the Last Day: "The power of the Holy Spirit . . . shows and promises the dawn of this day, proclaiming it in his operation and already being to him (the Christian) the pledge and earnest of its coming (Rom 8:23) and therefore of the nearness of his

redemption."[41] This hope enables us to continue in persever-
ence and faithfulness despite appearances to the contrary. It
gives us the assurance of final victory and the confidence to
meet the coming Judge. It means also that the real end towards which we move is not merely death or the end otherwise of this temporal existence, but the great day of the
Lord, a day of joy leading to a life "of exaltation to the eternal light of eternal life."[42]

If we have this sure hope it can be no mere individual affair, nor will it be a hope purely for the future,—an
impossibility anyway. This future hope will lead to proximate hopes and corresponding action and—though not specifically mentioned here action not only by the individual
or in the Christian community, but action by the Christian
and the community in the social and political realm as well,
for Barth saw all life as one. We will experience and see
small lights in the present darkness reflecting the God of
light and hope and the Christian will live a prophetic existence, that is, one that points forward in hope and one that
exercises itself in the present by the power of the Holy
Spirit. This again is a gift from God but is at the same time
our own action. It is by the Holy Spirit alone; but in so giving it gives us spontaneous freedom to act though never
giving itself over into our control. Nevertheless, it is "the
Spirit who creates hope and therefore the Christian can
only daily pray anew for hope."[43]

D. CRITIQUE OF OTHER VIEWS

There are three areas where Barth is in clear disagreement with the views of others.

a) Roman Catholicism teaches that since the Scriptures with tradition interpreted by the *Magisterium* (the
bishops in their teaching office) rightly decide what is to be
received and believed, the faithful are to accept this with
implicit faith. Faith is of course also directed to Christ as
the sole Mediator but who he is and how he is to be understood are only properly interpreted as stated above. Hence

implicit obedience to this authority is a true expression of real faith.

For Barth, on the contrary, the ultimate authority is God speaking in his Word and faith is acknowledgment of this, a true acknowledgment of God in Christ and of oneself in him. The Church helps to formulate this faith but its word can never be accepted as if it were almost identical with God's. That a human word becomes the Word of God is, for Barth, always the event of God's action by the Holy Spirit.

b) The believing individual can and does correspond to Christ in the Christian life through dying and rising with him but he does not and cannot repeat or represent Christ. Barth has a threefold thrust in view here.[44]

> Against R. Bultmann, who sees humanity responding to Christ through the kerygma where it makes the cross of Christ its own or, to put it otherwise, the cross becomes reality in one's living and dying.
>
> Against Roman Catholicism as represented by Hans Urs von Balthasar, who sees the saints as reproducing, reflecting or re-enacting the history of Jesus Christ in such a way that Christ himself fades into the background. But Barth asks "whether in all the spiritual splendour of the saints who are supposed to represent and repeat him Jesus Christ has not ceased not in theory but in practice—to be the object and origin of Christian faith."[45]
>
> Against Oscar Cullmann,[46] whose doctrine of baptism of infants makes it, in Barth's opinion, tantamount to a second salvation event.

For Barth, however, "faith is the free act of man, and is wonderful enough in relationship to Jesus Christ as its object and origin. It is a recognition and apprehension of his being and activity for man. But it is not the repetition of it."[47] In this Barth is surely right against both Roman Catholic and Protestant misrepresentations. He writes again, "If only we were agreed—and this applies to my neighbour on the left (Existentialist Protestantism) as well as on the right

(Roman Catholicism)—that the ultimate and penultimate things, the redemptive act of God and that which passes for our response to it, are not the same. Everything is jeopardized if there is confusion in this respect."[48] What one can posit (and Barth does this repeatedly) is a correspondence or analogy between our actions in faith and life and God's action in Christ for our redemption. But there should be no identity, confusion or repetition. Rather, as Barth states,

> "The real presentation (*repraesentatio*) of the history of Jesus Christ is that which he himself accomplishes in the work of his Holy Spirit when he makes himself the object and origin of faith."[49]
> "The Spirit alone is the mediator between . . . the redemptive act of God and man's free response to it . . . Because the divine being and work of the Holy Spirit mediate between Christ and the Christian, his presence and activity are operative at both poles. He is the Spirit of the atonement *extra nos* in Jesus Christ and also the Spirit of the atonement's 'existential reach' *in nobis*."[50]

c) The relationship between faith and love: Roman Catholicism teaches that faith is formed by love—*fides caritate formata*. It is formed and penetrated by our love of God in such a way that love almost becomes the cause of faith rather than Jesus Christ. Moreover it also means that one has to wait until this faith is formed by love before one is justified. In other words, there is a confusion between justification and sanctification.

For the Reformers and for Barth, on the contrary, while faith and love go together faith is formed by Christ and is active in and produces love; it works by it. Rudolf Ehrlich puts the difference in this way, "Of course the justified sinner loves God. But they (the Reformers) utterly reject the Roman view that the person justified by faith has to love God in order to be justified. Christ and Christ alone justifies—not love; not even the most sublime love of man can obtain for him the forgiveness of sins—only grace, which is Christ, can do it and does it. Man does not love so as to be justified, he loves because he is justified."[51]

E. SUMMARY AND EVALUATION

In the very last pages of Vol. IV/3, 2 of the *Church Dogmatics*[52] Barth gives a fine summary of his position with an implicit reply to his critics. In this he emphasises that the work of the Holy Spirit is God's work and not ours and that the holiness of the Spirit points to the freedom of God.

In this Barth is underlining both the freedom and the sovereignty of God to act as, when and where he pleases. He is in no way constrained to act. God is the *Holy* Spirit who acts in grace and judgment as Sovereign Lord. At the same time he wills to and does recreate humanity, yet carries this out in a way which makes an individual a free, active subject, willingly responding to God's offer in Christ, receiving the Holy Spirit as the power of God's incarnate Word, his reconciliation. It is precisely in this way that a person is not only freed for God but freed from sin's self-alienation and becomes truly human. Negatively, this means that God does not override human personality, acting as a kind of arbitrary power forcing our submission. Positively, it signifies that he so acts as to remain free himself while creating free, spontaneous faith, love and hope.

In the whole of Vol.IV, part 2, of the *Church Dogmatics,* Barth is seeking to give his own answer to a question that faces all theology, namely, what part (if any) does humanity play in its own salvation? The answer of the Churches of the Reformation is clear. Salvation is God's act in Christ to which humanity, because of the bondage of the will (*servum arbitrium*), can contribute nothing. It is all of God and of his grace and humanity can only be a passive recipient; even this possibility is God's gift of grace. This answer Barth accepts and repeats but takes it a step further since it leaves unanswered the question—what is the meaning of the act of faith, love and hope which is clearly also

our own activity? The Roman Catholic answer tends to be
that all is of grace and Christ is the only Mediator and Saviour. But, at the same time, humanity is able to contribute as
a secondary cause or subject; human bondage is not so
complete that the individual is merely passive. Or, more
correctly, one is given the ability to co-operate with Christ
and so oneself play a part.

Colin O'Grady encapsulates perfectly in a few brief
sentences the basic difference between Reformation and
Roman Catholic doctrine at this point. He writes, "The doctrine of the Catholic Church and the doctrine of Karl Barth
agree on the fundamental point: justification is originally
and primarily God's gracious act alone. They also agree in
many other points. But Barth disagrees with us on this
equally fundamental point: while God is the sole ultimate
subject, he is not the sole subject of justification.

The Christian is also its subject. Not just a subject
in justification, but, in complete dependence on God, a subject of justification."[53] This means that the human act of
faith is for Roman Catholics "the necessary condition of
justification, or salvation."[54] For Barth and Reformation
doctrine faith is the way grace comes and is received but
cannot be its precondition in any sense.

Barth, in line with the Reformers, rightly rejects the
Catholic answer since, though it seems to place all the emphasis on grace, at the same time leaves a loophole for humanity acting in what appears to be a semi-independent
way. If this is a wrong way of answering the question,
Barth, nonetheless, believes that the question is there and
requires an answer. Though, at this point, one is near to the
danger of the answer of Roman Catholicism and Liberal
Protestantism (even some aspects of Evangelicalism) one
cannot evade the issue. The answer Barth gives is essentially a christological and pneumatological one. God is not a
God in abstraction from but is the God revealed in Jesus
Christ. In him God and humanity are one; God the Son
humbling himself to us and humanity at the same time exalted. In this union and exaltation humanity is truly itself, in
a sense, a secondary subject in the act of reconciliation. It

is, therefore primarily in Christ that humanity acts as subject in reconciliation. But, in union with Christ we are made truly human, exercise a royal freedom and by the Holy Spirit become subjects of our own action in a way which does not threaten the Lordship of Christ but serves and testifies to it.

Barth's treatment is, *therefore*, an attempt to deal with questions answered differently by Roman Catholics, Liberal Protestants and Pietists. He writes, "I hope that in relation to Roman Catholic theology some contribution has been made to an understanding of what is there called 'sanctifying grace'. It is another question whether on our side I have even remotely satisfied the concerns of the Pietists and 'Evangelical groups'. To the best of my knowledge and conscience I have tried to do this, although I could not simply adopt their view."[55] He could not adopt their view for the reason that they tended to place too great emphasis on the subjective experience of Christ rather than on Christ himself and because they appealed to a human decision which, while attributed to the Holy Spirit, seemed too much like our own work. It was this danger in all its forms that Barth sought vigorously to counter not only by denial but more importantly by his own positive re-statement. This re-statement at the same time attempted to include the positive intentions of his opponents. The same thing had to be said but said differently.

NOTES

1. *C.D.*, II/1, p.158.
2. Ibid.
3. Ibid.
4. *C.D.*, IV/1, p. 740.
5. Ibid., p. 748.
6. Ibid., p. 751.

7. Ibid., p. 754.

8. Ibid., p. 758.

9. Calvin, *Institutes*, I, 6, 2.

10. *C.D.*, IV/1, pp. 767-768. This is discussed more fully later.

11. Rosato, *The Spirit as Lord*, p. 115.

12. Op.cit., p. 776.

13. Ibid., p. 753.

14. *C.D.*, IV/2, p. 730.

15. Ibid., p. 731.

16. Rudolf J. Ehrlich, *Rome, Opponent or Partner?* London: Lutterworth Press, 1965, p. 89.

17. Ibid.

18. Ibid.

19. *C.D.*, IV/2, p. 737; cf. however, *C.D.*, III/2, pp. 274-285, where the sharp distinction is somewhat modified by an emphasis on our common humanity.

20. See chapter II, above.

21. *C.D.*, IV/2, pp. 778-779.

22. Otto Weber, *Karl Barths Kirchliche Dogmatik*, Neukirchener Verlag, Damstadt 6th Edltion, 1963, p. 280. (*Karl Barth's Church Dogmatics*).

23. *C.D.*, IV/2, p. 785.

24. Ibid.

25. Ibid., p. 788.

26. Ibid., p. 795f.

27. John A. T. Robinson, *Honest to God*, London: S.C.M., 1963, pp. 45ff.

28. Cf. *C.D.*, II/1, pp. 257ff.

29. *C.D.*, IV/2, p. 800.

30. Ibid., p. 802.

31. Ibid. At first sight it seems strange, indeed wrong, to hear Barth speak of the neighbour as primarily the Christian brother and sisterwithin the covenant. On the meaning of "neighbour" in the Bible it has been written, "Modern man, especially since the Enlightenment, is mostly inclined to think that the neighbour is simply one's fellow-man" [*Theological Dictionary of the New Testament*, Gerhard Kittel ed., Grand Rapids: Wm. B. Eerdmans, 1968, trs. Geoffey W. Bromiley, Vol

VI . pp. 311- 318.] However, the same writer points out that in the Old and New Testaments "neighbour" is chiefly associated with those nearest, i.e., those possibly within the covenant relationship. But, at the same time, as Barth states, this broadens out to envisage and embrace all humanity. In the light of the biblical understanding Barth is essentially correct in contrast to a general humanistic view influenced, to a large extent, by the general ethos in society.

32. Op.cit., p. 282.
33. *C.D.*, IV/2, p. 809.
34. Ibid., p. 818.
35. Ibid., p. 525.
36. Ibid., p. 529.
37. Ibid., p. 533.
38. J. Lesslie Newbigin, *The Household of God*, London: S.C.M.1953, p. 25.
39. *C.D.*, IV/3, 2, p. 911.
40. Ibid., p. 916.
41. Ibid.
42. Ibid., p. 928.
43. Otto Weber, op.cit., p. 330.
44. *C.D.*, IV/l, pp. 767-769 .
45. Ibid., p. 768.
46. Ibid., cf. Oscar Cullmann, *Baptism in the New Testament*, trs. J. K. S. Reid, London: S.C.M., 1950. In Barth's Seminar in Basel 1947-48 he criticised Cullmann for making Baptism virtually a second salvation—event—a representation of Christ's baptism.
47. Ibid., pp. 768-769.
48. Ibid., p. 768.
49. Ibid., p. 767 .
50. Rosato, op.cit., p. 115.
51. Ehrlich, op.cit., p. 89.
52. *C.D.*, IV/3, 2, pp. 941-942.
53. Colin O'Grady, *The Church in Catholic Theology; Dialogue with Karl Barth*, Vol. II, London: Geoffrey Chapman, 1969 p. 244.
54. Ibid., p. 248.
55. *C.D.*, IV/2, p. x.

CHAPTER NINE

THE HOLY SPIRIT, CREATION AND HUMANITY

We have seen that the theology of Karl Barth is wholly christocentric in character. Can it be that in the doctrines of creation and of humanity we are in a different realm? Have we here, as some might think, "a sort of 'forecourt' of the Gentiles, a realm in which Christians and Jews and Gentiles, believers and unbelievers are beside one another and to some extent stand together in the presence of a reality concerning which there might be some measure of agreement, in describing it as the work of God the Creator?"[1] Barth's reply to this is an emphatic *no*, since here we are not in the region of general ideas about God, of a world-view shared with others, but within the sphere of Christian revelation and faith. In other words, we do not begin with a general view of God which would lead us to affirm that he made the world and then go on to posit belief in Jesus Christ on the basis of revelation and the biblical witness to it. On the contrary, as the creeds themselves clearly affirm, belief in God as Creator and the world as his creation is an article of faith—a *credo*—I (we) believe "It is not the case that the truth about God the Creator is directly accessible to us and that only the truth of the second article needs a revelation. But in the same sense in both cases we are faced with the mystery of God and his work, and the approach to it can only be one and the same."[2]

A . THE CHRISTOLOGICAL BASIS

What Barth is affirming is that the knowledge we have here is an integral part of Christian knowledge and confession. What he is speaking against is a form of "natural" theology which presupposes some other source or form of such knowledge. His position can be stated in several ways:

a) Revelation.

It is as God reveals himself and reconciles us to himself in Jesus Christ that by faith we apprehend him. We know him as Lord and Saviour, as Son who points us to his father and ours—the one who made us and not we ourselves. As in the Old Testament so in the New, faith in God as Creator is an implicate of revelation and our knowledge of the Son. It has this christological basis.

Barth can and does state this more specifically by showing that in Jesus Christ we have at one and the same time knowledge of who God is as Creator and what humanity is as creature. The clue to the knowledge of God, humanity and creation he finds therefore in the incarnation.[3] By revelation through faith we perceive that in Jesus Christ we meet with God who, although perfect in himself and the source of all that is, at the same time exists in partnership with that which is not God, with humanity and creation. In Jesus Christ we know the reality of God and the reality of that which is different from God and yet is his work, namely, the creature. In the man Jesus we know that this and all other creaturely reality owes its being and continuing existence to God. It is not God, not eternal, nor a mere appearance, but has true, distinct reality in its relationship to God in Jesus Christ.

In this union of God and humanity in Jesus Christ we have the one sure way of knowing who God is and what humanity is both in their relationship and distinction as Lord and Creator on the one hand and as dependent creature on the other. Barth calls this its *noetic* side—the way we know this truth about God, ourselves and, (implicit in this), our world.[4] At the same time Jesus Christ is the *ontic* basis of this, i.e., he is the reality of it, the one who is the basis of its actuality. In other words it is through him we understand that the worlds were framed by the Word of God (Heb. 1:3), since he is that Word made flesh, existing in creaturely form. Jesus Christ is both the basis and goal of creation. All things are through him, by him, and for him: without him nothing could be made, "for in him all things were created in heaven and on earth . . . all things were created through him and for him. He is before all things and in him all things cohere." (Col 1:15-18) Therefore we can and must say—the Word first, the world second, what Barth calls, "a marvellous reversal of our whole thinking."[6] He can even go so far as to say, "the world came into being, it was created and sustained by the little child that was born in Bethlehem, by the man who died on the cross of Golgotha, and the third day rose again."[7] By this we are to understand not a child or man as such but the child and man who, as creaturely reality, is one with the eternal Word, the man Christ Jesus.

b) Creation and Covenant

The reversal in thinking which Barth calls upon us to make is nowhere more clearly seen than in his conception of the relation of creation to covenant. Since Jesus Christ, the Reconciler, is the fulfillment of Israel's history and of God's action in it he is the meaning and content of the covenant. The covenant is the center and key to creation —its inner ground. On the other hand creation is the outer ground or basis of the covenant. In fact creation comes, and with it space and time, before the historical realization of the covenant but, in reality, in the eternal will and purpose of God covenant precedes creation. In a lengthy exposition of the Genesis stories,[8] which he regards not as myth but as Saga[9] Barth seeks to show how, while these accounts "lie outside of our historical knowledge," nonetheless they speak "upon the basis of knowledge which is related to history."[10] In other words they stand in immediate relationship to the succeeding history of God's covenant with Israel. In the Genesis accounts the covenant is the goal of creation in pointing to the institution of the Sabbath and the subsequent history of God's action. But, in the light of this action, the creation is seen as setting the stage for the covenant of grace which was in God's eternal will from the beginning and is the purpose of creation itself.[11] God's gracious reconciliation of humanity in and through the covenant relationship is thus no "afterthought" consequent upon the Fall, but is the original will of God for humanity. Creation is thus, in Calvin's words, the sphere of the glory of God, (*theatrum gloriae Dei*)[13]—a glory which culminates and is fully manifest in Jesus Christ.

c) Creation as Grace[14]

Creation is not something based on an inner necessity of deity or on anything outside God. It has its basis in his freedom, will and decision to be the God of humanity to give to "another" outside himself a relative independence and reality. Indeed Barth sees this as "the great puzzle and miracle . . . That there is a world is the most unheard-of thing, the miracle of the grace of God."[15] The real mystery is thus not so much that God exists but that we do, that, alongside himself, he actually created a world and us within it. So, with Luther, we can say that creation is grace. In so acting, giving creation and us existence God acted freely and willingly, not grudgingly or reluctantly. We exist and heaven and earth exist because of the gift of God's grace and because he continually says "Yes" to his work, affirms creation and his creatures.

One can say that, basically, this goodness and mercy are a kind of a reflex of God's grace in Christ. Since, from all eternity, in the counsel of his will he has had mercy on us and has revealed and effected this in Jesus Christ we know that all God's ways and works with us have this sure basis: "Creation is understood and apprehended as grace in faith in Jesus Christ."[16]

d) Creation and the Trinity

Creation is not only christologically based but, because it is so, it has a trinitarian basis. This is seen in three ways.

First, it is the work of God who is triune. The revelation that he is such and acts in this way humanity (which is also sinful knows through God's reconciliation in Jesus Christ. It is the Son who reveals the Father and it is both Father and Son who send the Spirit. Barth can say with "the older Protestant dogmaticians" (Melanchthon, Bucanus, Polanus and J. Gerhard) that creation is "the work of the whole Trinity."[17] It is right and indeed necessary to speak in this way, not only because God is so, but also because the inner relationships in God as Father, Son and Holy Spirit have, as we shall see, significance for the varied relationships between creation and covenant.

Secondly, as in the Creed, creation is specifically ascribed to the Father—"the Almighty, maker of heaven and earth". This is so because what God does in his works *ad extra* (outside himself) reflects and corresponds to what he is in himself. In the triune life the Father is the source of the Son eternally and with the Son of the Holy Spirit. It is therefore appropriate that he should be specially, though not exclusively, referred to as the Creator.[18]

Thirdly, a very characteristic emphasis of Barth's is that God creates by the Word or Son. But since from all eternity God has decided and willed to be the God of humanity in Jesus Christ and to unite himself with us "that in his person he should bear and bear away the curse of sin for all men,"[19] the connection between creation and covenant becomes clear and unmistakable. In Christ God not only created the world and humanity but loved it and us even before their creation. It is indeed this love that was to redeem that is the basis of his act of creation.

Thus we can see that the Trinity, creation and redemption are closely related in Barth's thought. Creation is a gracious act of the divine love of the triune God—a love revealed in the reconciliation of sinful humanity in Jesus Christ.

e) Creation and The Holy Spirit

What we have already stated of the Trinity (in more general terms) must now be related specifically to the Holy Spirit and its role. For Barth (closely following Augustine) the Holy Spirit is the communion of Father and Son, their mutual self-giving to one another in love. At the same time the Spirit is personal and together with the Father and the Son equally divine. In fact God would not be God without the Spirit nor would we know it to be such. It is in and through the Spirit that one knows the distinction of the persons from one another and their relatedness to one another as well as their unity as divine. The Spirit is therefore the principle of the inner, divine, triune life of God. "To this extent it may well be said that it is in the Holy Spirit that the mystery of God's trinitarian essence attains its full profundity and clarity."[20]

This mystery revealed by the Spirit can be put in this way. The Spirit is not only the communion and mutual self-impartation of Father and Son in the divine life but is, as such, the self-affirmation of God. It is in this way that God is God. The Holy Spirit is, as we have seen, the One who focusses the whole divine activity *ad extra*—towards humanity and creation, "the whole order of the relation between God the Creator and his creatures."[21] As the Spirit affirms the triune nature of God so, analogous to this, it confirms and guarantees what God has done in creation. One can say, therefore, that already in the divine life the Holy Spirit is the guarantor both of all created being and of our continued existence.

The relationship between the triune God and creation can be put in this way. God the Father is the Creator, God the Son, the means and goal of creation, God the Holy Spirit, the one who particularly guarantees its existence: "For that reason it is only in the Holy Spirit that the creature can be sure that it can and may exist."[22] This should not be taken as in any way querying the creation of the world by God through the Son but rather the confirmation by God that what he has made he affirms and maintains in being. It is the confirmation and guarantee of its validity in the will and purpose of the Father and the Son. The Holy Spirit performs no separate work but this distinctive work which is also the indivisible work of the whole Trinity.

Barth states that the Bible nowhere speaks of the world as created by the Spirit. Nonetheless we cannot exist without it. Since the Spirit is agent and communion of Father and Son and since God the Father and the Son are one and creation is their work, the Spirit is "the *conditio sine qua non* of the creation and preservation of the creature."[23]

At the same time Barth argues from reconciliation to creation, from covenant to its outer ground. In reconciliation the Spirit is the Spirit of Christ crucified and risen for our salvation. But the same Lord is the agent of creation. Therefore the Spirit is also involved as pointing to the sure work and basis in the Son and Father; indeed the One who brings us reconciliation subjectively also confirms creation. We know this work from the Son retrospectively and indirectly as testifying that "there could be no creature, nor any creation, if God were not also the Holy Spirit and active as such."[24] In other words if the Spirit is the Spirit of the Father and the Son and if we know creation through reconciliation—reconciliation is ours through the Spirit—the Spirit is also the indispensable link in the word and work of creation. The ground of creation is the Word incarnate and the Spirit is his Spirit; hence without the Spirit the work of the Word would be void.

B. HUMANITY AS CREATURE

The center and goal of creation is humanity; the true nature of humanity cannot, however, be read off from human nature since it has fallen and is out of true relationship with God. It is this true relationship of fellowship and love that constitutes our true humanity. The only place where this can be seen is in the man Christ Jesus. Anthropology is, therefore, based on christology and is not to be read off from any general conceptions we may have of humanity however right these may be in their own limited way. Humanity is God's creature whose relation to God is revealed in his Word: "As the man Jesus is himself the revealing Word of God, he is the source of our knowledge of the nature of man as created by God."[25] Therefore, argues Barth, "we must really keep to the human nature of Jesus. Thus we may not deviate from it, nor may we on any account rely upon, nor take for granted, what we think we know about man from other sources. We must form and maintain the conviction that the presupposition given us in and with the human nature of Jesus is exhaustive and superior to all other presuppositions, and that all other presuppositions can become possible and useful only in connexion with it."[26] It must, however, be made clear that Barth regards the humanity of Jesus, as does traditional orthodoxy, as constituted by the Word. It has no existence as such save as it is assumed into union with the Word; at the same time in this union it has particular, individual life so that one can speak of the one man Jesus Christ. In speaking of the man Jesus who is also representative humanity and in seeking here to show his relationship to the Holy Spirit this context must never be forgotten.

Yet it is also true that in Christian thinking and doctrine we can, for the sake of clarity and exposition, look at the humanity of Jesus for a moment on its own. When we do so two things emerge; this man Jesus is a unity of soul and body in this distinction and order.[27] At the same time and as such he stands in a special relationship to the Holy Spirit: "We have here to regard this relationship as the particular determination of the human constitution of Jesus."[28] At this point theology has generally said that Jesus is a man who receives and bears the Spirit.

In Barth's theology Jesus is the royal man exalted by union with the divine to fulfil a kingly office. Accordingly, he sees the Spirit as the kingly Spirit in the line of David marking Jesus out as the true Messiah: "He is to be a man who is pervasively and constantly, intensively and totally filled and governed by this kingly Spirit."[29] He is conceived and brought into being by the same Spirit so that we can say: "the relationship of this man to the Holy Spirit is so close and special that he owes no more and no less than his existence itself and as such to the Holy Spirit."[30] But in the Old and New Testaments the Holy Spirit is "God himself in his creative movement to his creation."[31] To others of his creatures the Spirit comes from time to time; with Jesus the Spirit abides: "He is the man to whom the creative

movement of God has come primarily, originally and therefore definitively."[32] In comparison with others his is a quite
unique relationship to the Spirit; we cannot say that our life
is in the same permanent and intimate relationship to the
Spirit as that of Jesus. The man Jesus is created and remains the true and royal, the new and reconciled man and
as such has an eternal inheritance. Because he is one of us
yet in this way superior to us in perfection by the Spirit—
"the perfect Recipient and bearer of the Spirit"[33]—he is the
prototype and guarantor of our true humanity and eternal
life.

Thus we can say that the fullness of the Spirit of
God addressed by God to the creature dwells in Jesus as
man and is his very life, making his passage through Gali-
lee and Jerusalem in all its humility and suffering a royal
and triumphant procession to his victory and ours. As man
we can see him conforming perfectly to the Father's will; in
him was life. He is, therefore, the perfect exemplar of what
we ought and are to be—conformed to the image and likeness of God. If, therefore, we wish to see the way and work
of God by his Spirit with his creatures and particularly with
humanity we see this in its perfection and fulness in the
man Christ Jesus. Humanity made to be like God has in
Christ that perfect reflection.

Because he is man whose whole existence is an existence in and by the Spirit he is the only Holy One.[34] Yet
our calling is to be like him, to be the holy ones, to be
"saints,"[35] to be sanctified. How is this transition to come
about in us from sin to holiness? The answer is, by the
Holy Spirit. Barth argues[36] that, since the Son of God in union with the Son of Man has reconciled the world to himself, he has *de jure* included us all in his holy humanity.
But, despite this, we still remain sinners and have to be incorporated into him, lifted up to where he is, given this
thrust and direction. Negatively,[37] this happens when we
are *de facto* disturbed in our sloth and disobedience and
positively[38] exalted to where he is. Thus by the Holy Spirit
we are not only set in a right relation with God but are
changed in our very being,[39] becoming what we are already

in Christ—the saints—the holy people of God, the true and
exalted human beings, reflecting the holy life of Christ. In
this way we receive and have a decisive freedom to obey.

C. HUMANITY IN THE IMAGE OF GOD

Barth's earlier teaching[40] was that though God created humanity in his image, our fallen state meant that the
image was entirely destroyed. But the grace of God could
and did restore humanity to the likeness of God and his purpose for us. Later in the *Church Dogmatics*[41] his view of the
image changed; he saw our created nature as being in the
image of God—which had never been lost even by sin. The
image does not, therefore, consist in a quality in humanity
which could be destroyed or lost but in what might be
called a "structured relationship". Barth teaches that in the
relationship between man and woman, an "I" and "Thou",
we see a likeness to God who is not isolated or lonely but a
being-in-relationship. In other words in his theology he
combines two ideas which become prominent and important features of it, namely, the doctrines of the image of
God and of analogy. But since Barth's whole theology is
christological and trinitarian we must now show how these
are related to this central theme.

Basing his position on an exposition of Genesis
1:27,[42] Barth seeks to show that it is this relationship of
man and his creaturely being to a partner women that is the
image of God in humanity. This is not a form of natural
theology; it is not a point of contact in humanity which can
only be created by the Holy Spirit but a structured relationship in which humanity is human and reflects a relationship
in God. Since humanity is such it is only a "sign"[43] and this
sign is only known in its true nature and meaning in Jesus
Christ. This christological basis we must now briefly eluci-
date. God has entered into covenant with humanity in Israel
and in Jesus Christ. In him he has elected humanity to fellowship with himself to reflect his glory. Since Jesus Christ
is the man for others and is at the same time one with God,

the one man in his totality for all humanity, he is the image of God in its truth and reality. The image is thus seen and known in the humanity of Jesus Christ who at one and the same time is Son of God and reveals God to us as Father, Son and Holy Spirit. God is thus one who is in mutual relationship, co-existence and coinherence in and with himself. Barth puts it like this, "Man has plurality like God, who is plural. Being man means being in togetherness: man and wife. 'Living God' means 'togetherness'. This togetherness is, according to Ephesians, Christ and his Church: the *eikon*. Image has a double meaning: God lives in togetherness with himself, then God lives in togetherness with man, then men live in togetherness with one another. The middle term is the foundation of man's likeness to God: togetherness in relation, and proceeding out of these is an analogy."[44] In other words it is in and through the union and communion of God and humanity in Jesus Christ (the middle term) that we know the nature of humanity and its likeness to God. In him too we know true being in relationship; in him too we know that being for others is the very nature of the humanity of Christ, the image of God in us. In this light we see the purpose of God for us as human beings in true relationship with our fellows. But this nature of our humanity and all these relationships are perceived in and through faith in Jesus Christ.

One could sum this up by saying that image has a prototype in God to which there is a correspondence in God's relationship to the world and in our creaturely being in the world. The counterpart to God himself has at least a twofold correspondence (a) in the co-existence of God and humanity; (b) in our independent existence where we are related to our fellows. There is an "I" and a "Thou" in God, and an "I" and a "Thou" in Jesus Christ, in his divinity and humanity, an "I" and a "Thou" in male and female. Our humanity in Christ and so in us as co-humanity is the image of God. Our humanity therefore has the nature and possibility of partnership; *imago dei* is the very nature of our creatureliness and so cannot be lost by the Fall. Thus in its very being humanity reflects God. It cannot be an analogy of being (*analogia entis*) as in Roman Catholicism where God and humanity have something in common. It is rather an analogy perceived by faith *analogia fidei,* and furthermore one of several relationships *analogia relationis.* It is thus not a correspondence of likes but an analogy of dissimilars, since humanity is not similar to God in being but only in certain relationships. These are illumined in Christ and not perceived *per se* or naturally. Futhermore, though the image of God is seen in humanity and in our nature as such, it is only possible for us to exercise it fully when by the Holy Spirit we are elevated to a new birth, reborn as members of Christ's body and in this relationship we are able to be for others—in the image of God.

D. Humanity AS BODY AND SOUL

We begin with the thesis Barth sets out to expound here: "Man exists because he has spirit. That he has spirit means that he is grounded, constituted and maintained by God as the soul of his body."[45] Barth argues first, negatively, that though humanity is creature and not divine it is not and could not be without God. Positively, however, humanity has its basis, constitution and continued existence from God. More specifically its being has an inner relationship to God's turning to us, to God's grace and salvation. Creation and the covenant are so intimately and irrevocably related that humanity "is determined by the one grace, that of his creation, for the other grace, that of the covenant."[46] The same theme which pervades Barth's whole doctrine of creation and humanity is explicitly stated again in a new context.

Humanity has a twofold existence as body and soul. It is the soul of a body. That it is and can exist as such in this organic yet ordered union comes about by "the free act of God", his "free creative grace."[47] "His act alone is the event in which the reality of human being and human existence, the soul of the body, can arise and remain."[48] To put it otherwise, humanity exists as it has spirit. Barth rejects the view of humanity as three-fold-body, soul and spirit and believes the biblical doctrine envisages a twofold nature of humanity as body and soul. But since spirit is spoken of in relation to humanity Barth believes this means the divine spirit, the Holy Spirit of the Father and the Son. Humanity is as it has this spirit; it is by the Spirit that our human being is constituted. One cannot therefore say humanity is, but rather it has spirit.

Again, one must underline the relationship of human nature to grace; it is not a natural movement from one to the other, but one based on the reality of grace. Just as God chooses and determines humanity to be his, to be a "new" creation and live in fellowship with him by giving the Holy Spirit of his reconciling grace, so, on this basis, he at one and the same time by the same Spirit makes possible and guarantees the being and the continued existence of humanity as creaturely. This creaturely existence Barth sees related to the covenant and reconciliation as "presupposition" and "promise".[49] Humanity exists, since without it God cannot have a creaturely covenant partner, but humanity exists as promise since it is determined and called to eternal fellowship and life with God as Creator, Reconciler and Redeemer. It is the Holy Spirit who is the life both of humanity in its creaturely existence as soul of the body and as reconciled, man. In this anthropological sphere "to have Spirit means that he may live, and therefore be soul, and therefore be soul of his body."[50]

Barth draws all this together in four brief affirmations.[51]

a) God is there for us in free grace as Creator; humanity has no divine part but is wholly creaturely.

b) To have Spirit is what makes us human, the decisive determination of our being.

c) The Spirit is in humanity in the most intimate way as principle of its existence but is not identical with it.

d) The Spirit acts on the soul and through it on the body, "It is as the principle of the soul that the Spirit is the principle of the whole man."[52]

E. CRITIQUE AND EVALUATION

There is wide agreement, even amongst those critical of Barth, that his doctrine of creation and humanity is a very great theological achievement. David Cairns, himself critical of Barth on this issue, speaks for many when he writes, "It will probably be the verdict of later times that this is one of the greatest theological works of the last half century."[53] There are several points where Barth's exposition has a novel and original quality.

a) Christology and Anthropology

H. Hartwell writes, "Barth's doctrine of man is the most consistent one of its kind and is revolutionary in content."[54] By this he means that Barth has radically reversed traditional dogmatics which began with the phenomenon of the human, with our human being, and then went on to speak of the humanity of Jesus Christ. Barth reverses the order which is consistent with his basic christological emphasis. In this way the doctrine of humanity is not deduced from but related to and interpreted in the light of the man Christ Jesus. In him we know who God is and what humanity is and in this light the nature of creation. We meet in the incarnation with their union and distinction. This basic christological thrust is, in my opinion, not only a valid but an illuminating one. The man Jesus is both one with God and yet is one with us as representative man. The character of our humanity and the nature of true humanity can be seen in him. In a rich variety of contexts Barth succeeds in drawing this out.

In other words we do not bring to our understanding of true humanity certain views of it which predetermine our conclusions nor do we deny these a relative validity. Rather we judge all these and evaluate them in the light of Jesus Christ and his humanity.

b) The Image of God in Humanity and Analogy

Here again Barth has made a unique contribution to the doctrine of the image of God in humanity and the nature of analogy related to it. His view that the image of God is a relationship of "I" and "Thou" reflecting the inner relationship of the triune God has not, however, found unanimous acceptance. J. J. Stamm[55] in summing up Old Testament scholarship from 1940-56 argues that three things are generally accepted: that the image includes both the physical and spiritual in humanity and that no definition which takes one or the other in isolation is adequate; in line with Barth the image is not something which can be lost since it is given in the nature of creation; it is not a quality of humanity which can be removed without us losing our humanity; in the context of the Old Testament faith Barth's position cannot be fully sustained though it cannot be completely denied. In the wider field of Scripture as a whole his is a possible solution and one which must be carefully considered.

On this basis it seems reasonable to state that Barth's position is at least a tenable one, especially when one thinks of the nature of humanity and community in the rest of the Scripture.

While it is true that Genesis 1:27 may not bear the whole weight of Barth's exegesis, it is also fair to add that he sees it in the perspective of the biblical witness as a whole, and in the context of his understanding of covenant and creation in particular. The two can be related in this way: the "I" and "Thou" of male and female is simply an indicator of our co-humanity as "I" and "Thou". The purpose of the creation of humanity made for partnership is that it may become the partner of God. Our created nature is thus in this relationship a "sign" pointing to the promise and possibility of a fellowship with God in covenant and reconciliation which God himself effects. This is not a point of contact for grace but its "natural" presupposition. One should also mention here that Barth's later writing on the "lights" and "truths" of creation, which can only be seen in their true nature through faith in Jesus Christ and in the fellowship of the Church, are similar to what he is saying here of the image of God in humanity.[56] Hence the analogy or correspondence to God and his action which the image in us displays is an analogy of faith (*analogia fidei*) and of relationship *(analogia relationis)* and not one of being *(analogia entis)* where there is a measure of similarity in being between God and humanity. It is therefore clear that with Barth christology and analogy go together as do his denial of natural theology and his affirmation of the nature of revelation and reconciliation.

c) The Holy Spirit and Humanity

A further original and fruitful aspect of Barth's exposition is his interweaving of the trinitarian, christological and anthropological aspects. The Holy Spirit is the one through whom we know God as he is since he is the communion of Father and Son. But the Father creates by the Word and in doing so he is not without the Spirit. The Spirit is thus the guarantor of our created existence since it affirms the nature of God and with it his action *ad extra*. Hence creation and we as creatures are both willed by God from all eternity and in time also created by him through the Word and sustained by the Holy Spirit.

It is the same Spirit who is the life of the one man Jesus the man for others, and for all humanity. It is the Spirit who gives us our ordered, structured, organic unity, a soul of our body. This threefold cord in Barth's doctrine of the Spirit and humanity is a fresh, new contribution to our understanding of God, the Holy Spirit and creation.

(d) The new position Barth represents has not passed without critical comment. G. S. Hendry makes three criticisms of Barth:

> 1) that the New Testament makes little reference to the Holy Spirit in creation; hence Barth's approach by which he deduces creation from the soteriological—eschatological work of the Spirit is dubious.[57] The context must not, however, be limited to the New Testament but seen in the light of the scripture witness as a whole. In this respect Barth's is a possible interpretation.
>
> 2) Barth identifies the Spirit, who is subjectively the principle of our renewal, with the Spirit as the principle of our creaturely reality thus evacuating the former of its specific subjective role.[58] The two, Hendry argues, cannot be prop-

erly combined. This again is doubtful since the Spirit is not
only the subjective reality of reconciliation but also one
with the Father and the Son in creation and preservation
and so has an ontic role.

3) More pertinent is Hendry's comment that to make the
Spirit the principle of our creaturely existence as body and
soul fails to clarify his relation to the Word who is the
agent of creation and the cohesive principle of the universe.[59] Does not the Spirit here tend to replace the Word?
Stock also questions Barth on this point by saying that "the
relationship of the dogmatic exegesis of Genesis 2:7 to the
trinitarian—theological discussion of the subject of the
creative act remains unclear."[60] Stock sees the exposition
of Barth's trinitarian basis for the Spirit's work in creation
as open to question. Barth sees the Spirit both as the power
which confirms the relationship of mutual love between
Father and Son in the triune life and at the same time as the
guarantee of our creaturely existence. But Stock writes:
"Barth does not show in what sense God's natural turning
(to man) should be called 'Spirit'."[61] There is a question
here which requires further elucidation as to how Word
and Spirit are related to man as soul and body.

It is interesting to note that Rosato, on the contrary,
speaks of Barth's writing on this point as "some of the most
profound pages of the *Church Dogmatics*" where "Barth
discusses the intradivine beginnings of all things, and in doing so grounds his entire pneumatology on his understanding of the role of the Spirit of God before the act of creation."[62]

One could summarize the relationship between the
Spirit, reconciliation and creation in Barth's theology in this
way. We know God because he has revealed himself to us
in Jesus Christ and this knowledge shows that it is exclusive in nature; it always at the same time reveals our incapacity. One cannot know Jesus Christ and therefore his humanity and therefore our's without the cross and and the
resurrection. They reveal the impossibility of human self-
knowledge attaining a knowledge of God; they show our

utter sinfulness and incapacity, yet at the same time they
manifest Christ as the key to God, humanity and creation.
The one who raises the dead by the Holy Spirit reaches out
to bring us into fellowship with himself. It is in the prophetic office of Christ which proclaims this act of reconciliation
in the power of the Holy Spirit that we know God both as
Reconciler and as Creator and so our true human nature.
Hence the Holy Spirit is the enabling power by which we
are not only reconciled but are also sure that we are the
creatures of God and are sustained by him. There can be no
direct way from sinful human nature to the God who is
known in reconciliation by the word of his work and in the
power of the Holy Spirit.

NOTES

1. Karl Barth, *Dogmatics in Outline*, trs. G. T. Thomson, London: S.C.M., 1949, p. 50.

2. Ibid., cf. *Credo*, trs. J. Strathern McNab, London: Hodder
and Stoughton, 1936, pp. 28-29; *C.D.*, III/1, p. 3.

3. *C.D.*, III/1, pp. 24-29.

4. Ibid., p. 28.

5. Ibid.

6. *Dogmatics in Outline*, p. 57,

7. Ibid., p. 58.

8. *C.D.*, III/1, pp. 94-329; cf. particularly pp. 94-97.

9. Myth is simply the retailing of inner-worldly realities and
problems. Saga is the story of God's action which embodies the truth
of his will (cf. the resurrection) but which is not susceptible of rational
proof by us; cf. *Dogmatics in Outline*, p. 51; *C.D.*, III/1, pp. 81f. It is
"an intuitive and poetic picture of a pre-historical reality of history
which is enacted once and for all within the confines of time and
space." (Ibid., p. 81).

10. *Dogmatics in Outline*, p. 51.

11. *C.D.*, III/1, p. 44. Konrad Stock points out that Rosato

starts out with the presupposition that Barth's anthropology is based on his pneumatology. This is only very partially true. In this way Rosato fails to see and underline the relationship between anthropology, covenant and reconciliation. See Stock, *Anthropologie der Verheissung, Karl Barths Lehre vom Menschen als dogmatisches Problem*, Munich: Chr. Kaiser Verlag, 1980, p. 156, n.2.

12. Ibid., p. 46.
13. *Dogmatics In Outline*, p. 58.
14. Ibid., p. 54; cf. *C.D.*, III/1, pp. 38-41.
15. Ibid.
16. *C.D.*, III/1, pp. 40-41.
17. Ibid., p.49.
18. Ibid.
19. Ibid., p. 50.
20. Ibid., p. 56.
21. Ibid. T. F. Torrance is critical of Barth's doctrine of creation which he says "did not offer an account of creation from an overarching trinitarian perspective," *How Karl Barth Changed My Mind.* p. 61. This is only very partially true, since, as we have seen, Barth definitely sets creation within a trinitarian context though possibly not a wholly overarching one.
22. Ibid., p. 57.
23. Ibid.
24. Ibid., p. 58.
25. *C.D.*, III/2, p. 3.
26. Ibid. p. 43.
27. Ibid., p. 325.
28. Ibid., p. 333.
29. Ibid.
30. Ibid.
31. Ibid.
32. Ibid., p. 334.
33. Ibid., p. 335.
34. *C.D.*, IV/2, p. 513.
35. Ibid., pp. 511ff.
36. Ibid., p. 521.
37. Ibid., p. 524f.
38. Ibid., p. 526f.

39. Ibid., p. 529. Barth writes, "it is a real alteration of their being."

40. *C.D.*, 1/1², p. 238f. cf. *The Knowledge of God and the Service of God*, p. 41f.

41. *C.D.*, III/1, pp. 183ff; *C.D.*, III/2, pp. 83f. pp. 323f.

42. *C.D.*, III/1, pp. 185ff.

43. *C.D.*, III/2, p. 322.

44. *Karl Barth's Table Talk*, (*T.T.*) Recorded and Edited by John D. Godsey, *Scottish Journal of Theology Occasional Papers*, No. 10, London and Edinburgh: Oliver & Boyd, 1963, p. 57.

45. *C.D.*, III/2, p. 344.

46. Ibid., p. 349.

47. Ibid., p. 351.

48. Ibid., p. 353.

49. Ibid., p. 360.

50. Ibid., p. 362.

51. Ibid., pp. 362-365.

52. Ibid., p. 365.

53. David Cairns, *The Image of God in Man*, London: S.C.M. 1953, p. 179. Stuart D. McLean, *Humanity in the Thought of Karl Barth*, Edinburgh: T. & T. Clark, 1981, writes, "My contention (is) that Barth's discussion of humanity is among the most profound in Western literature." (Ibid., p. vii)

54. H. Hartwell, *The Theology of Karl Barth: An Introduction*, London: Duckworth, 1964, p. 123.

55. J. J. Stamm. "Die Imago—Lehre von Karl Barth," *Antwort, Festschrift zum 70. Geburtstag von Karl Barth*, Zürich: Evangelischer Verlag, 1956, pp. 84-98. (The Image Doctrine of Karl Barth, *Answer, Tribute to Karl Barth on his seventieth birthday*). For a further full and fairly sympathetic discussion see Stock, op.cit., pp. 123-130. Stock believes that Barth's anthropology is too dominated by christology, that is, by its basis in the man Jesus rather than in God's creative Word (ibid., pp. 235-236). But is not the creative Word of God manifest in Jesus of Nazareth as the Son or Word of God? Gerhard von Rad in his commentary on Genesis I, trs. John H. Marks, London: S.C.M. 1961 pp. 57-58 indicates in a way close to Barth that the text speaks less of the nature than of the purpose of the image. Further, male and

female show a being for another in a community which reflects the being of the triune God.

56. Cf. John Thompson, *Christ in Perspective in the Theology of Karl Barth*, Edinburgh: The Saint Andrew Press, 1978, pp. 110-125.

57. G. S. Hendry, The Holy Spirit in Christian Theology, London: S.C.M., 1957, p. 50.

58. Ibid., p. 51; cf. Stock, op.cit., p. 157 for a similar verdict.

59. Ibid., p. 52.

60. Stock, op.cit., p. 161.

61. Ibid. cf. Ray S. Anderson, *On Being Human*, Grand Rapids: Wm B Eerdmans, 1982, p. 211 for a similar reservation.

62. Rosato, op.cit., p. 105. As over aginst both Hendry and Stock, Rosato sees Barth's view as having a proper trinitarian and pneumatological basis.

CHAPTER TEN

THE HOLY SPIRIT, ESCHATOLOGY AND THE CHRISTIAN LIFE

Eschatology, "the doctrine of the last things" has traditionally come at the end of systems of doctrine.[1] It was concerned with such subjects as heaven, hell, death and judgment, the resurrection, the consummation and God's ultimate reign. It often dealt more with the individual than with the future of the Church, mankind or the cosmos.

A dramatic change has taken place in this century in the thinking and writing about eschatology. While its significance as speaking of the "end" has not been queried or lessened it has been seen as speaking more about the "Eschatos, "the last one," Jesus Christ, rather than about the last things. In the more recent view his coming and action in history is and brings the end—the presence of God's purpose and its fulfilment amongst human beings. But history goes on. The question is then raised, how does the "End," or "Last One" at the heart of history affect our continuing life and our future hope? Various answers have been given including—the consequent eschatology of A. Schweitzer,[2] where the hope was for the End consequent upon Jesus' death; the "realised" eschatology of C.H. Dodd[3] with the End already realised in the kingdom come in Jesus and coming continually here and now; and a "futurist" eschatology represented by J. Moltmann,[4] where Jesus was simply the guarantor of the future end and not its full reality and meaning in history. Lastly there is the existentialist eschatology of Rudolf Bultmann,[5] where the End is seen as Christ meeting us in the kerygma (a kerygma influenced by a demythologised New Testament and a philosophical pre-understanding); the End is reached in our decision in relation to the cross and resurrection of Jesus, in our making the cross of Christ our own "now".

These ways of speaking about the Eschatos have seemed to some to fail to do justice to the fulness of the New Testament message. These other writers have presented a different view in an attempt to correct the imbalance—prominent among them Karl Barth.

A. THE ESCHATOLOGY OF KARL BARTH[6]

Barth's views come largely within the third aspect of the doctrine of reconciliation where Jesus Christ crucified, risen and reconciling proclaims himself by the Holy Spirit as the life and light of humanity. For Barth the "End" or "Last One" has come in Jesus Christ. Yet the New Testament speaks of three forms of this one event—past, present and to come, viz, the resurrection, the time of the Church and the final consummation.

In each and all of these "moments" it is the one Lord Jesus Christ who is present and expected. Yet it is the resurrection that is the definitive form of his appearing. Each other form will but confirm and manifest the reconciliation of Jesus Christ revealed in the resurrection. These other forms are the Holy Spirit and the Final Appearing or Second Coming. They can be called the first, middle and final forms. Like the Holy Trinity they are one but distinct in form yet coinhering in each other. In one respect, therefore, to speak of one is implicitly to speak of and include the others.

For our present purposes we limit ourselves to the middle form as Barth states it, i.e., the form of the Holy Spirit.

B. THE SPIRIT AND ESCHATOLOGY[7]

Jesus Christ as the Prophet of his own reconciliation

revealed in the resurrection declares with power to the world his own work by the Holy Spirit. The Holy Spirit is thus the power of the prophecy of Jesus Christ manifesting the glory of the Mediator. This time between the ages is no empty time when the Christian community is left on its own to await the final appearing. It is the day of the living Lord Jesus Christ in glorious power amongst men and women reaching out and including them in the saving purpose of God's will. Nor is it a time when the Christian community, deluded by a vain hope of the speedy Second Coming, looks forward with uncertainty. Rather it is a time filled with the power of the eschatos already manifest in Jesus Christ, inspiring eager expectancy and a hope always imminent. At the same time it also presses forward dynamically towards the visible manifestation of the great day of the Lord. In other words it is the positive fulness of what has come in Christ that determines our life now and our hope for the future.

This hope takes two forms—the presence of Jesus Christ by the Holy Spirit "as the One who promises and is promised."[8] Christ is the hope of all men—Christians and non-Christians alike—but in a different way; hence the two forms of the promise of the Spirit. This does not mean that the reality of faith or unbelief determines the attitude of Christ to us. Rather he is related to each in the same way as Lord of all yet in different ways since he is not recognised or accepted by all.

a) The Spirit Promises[9]

The Holy Spirit, or, alternately, "Jesus Christ acting and speaking in the power of the resurrection is present and active among and with and in certain men."[10] He is in and with his people, the community of faith. But, in being so, he guarantees to them the sure promise of redemption. Barth states the relation of the Holy Spirit to the resurrection and final appearance in this comprehensive way: "Jesus Christ in the power of his life as the Resurrected from the dead, in the glory of his coming again in its first form, gives to men the sure promise of his final appearing, of the conclusion of his revelation, and therefore of the redemption and perfecting of the world reconciled in him, of its participation in the life of this new cosmic form, and therefore of its own eternal life."[11] Here Barth says three things:

1. The basis of the promise is Jesus Christ in his glory as the Mediator risen from the dead.

2. On this basis he gives to his community the promise, by the Spirit's presence, of his final appearing at the end of the ages, of ultimate redemption.

3. This promise is the redemption or perfecting of the world in a scope which has significance not only for humanity but for the whole universe. Since we participate in and know this we have the guarantee of our own eternal life.

The Spirit who promises and is "not yet" is the Spirit present "already". It not only assures us of and guarantees the future goal but assists and is present with us now as we move towards this goal. We as Christians, "already" exist "in a distinctive way, as men who are determined and characterised by this promise . . . The promise of the Spirit sets them on the way to this end, and accompanies them on it."[12] It is thus on the basis of the first eschatos in the risen Christ and in the light of this final revelation that Christians live now, secure on this basis, enlightened and empowered by this presence and confirmed by a certain hope. They live as Christians reconciled but not yet redeemed. Barth underlines the dynamic impetus and movement of the Spirit's work not only in pointing to both basis and goal, beginning and end, but in enabling his community to move from one to the other. "In this sense Jesus Christ is here and now the hope of these men, of Christians."[13] It is in this light and for this purpose that he makes and keeps us Christians, that is, those who receive, bear and possess the promise of the Spirit and with it the understanding of its meaning and action.

b) The Spirit is Promised

Clearly the Holy Spirit as above described penetrating, indwelling and leading the people of God to a goal has not yet found reception in the lives of all; the Spirit is "still lacking and is still to be expected."[14] Both the ultimate goal and the proximate reality of being on the way are absent from many; not having the Holy Spirit they wander and go astray. Christ has included them in his reconciliation but they continue to exclude him; its *reality* for them has not become an *actuality* in them. Barth can say that "they will not yield their own spirits and wills and hearts and minds"[15] to the Spirit.

But, despite the fact that they have refused to yield and have closed themselves off from the Spirit, it is not absent from them and has not closed itself off from them; "For the Holy Spirit, as Jesus Christ is risen, is promised to them too"[16] as guarantee of the future and as presence here and now. They are, therefore, not condemned to a fate outside Christ either by what Christ has done or what is in themselves or what God imposes on them. Christ by the power of the Spirit is greater than they are, and his object is to come and meet them and overcome their resistance. One can say of each person in unbelief: "He, too, is reconciled to God. Jesus Christ died for him."[17] He rose and lives for this person too who on this basis and for this reason is also promised the Holy Spirit. Barth means by this that objectively Christ's death avails for all and therefore the promise of the Holy Spirit comes to all. What one must say of the unbeliever in relation to the Spirit is that the Spirit does not yet have this person. The "not yet" of faith by the Spirit pressing on towards the goal of the kingdom has its negative parallel in unbelief's "not yet" receiving and having the Holy Spirit. If the Spirit leads the believing community "on the way" to eternal life the same Spirit is also "on the way" to the unbeliever to bring that person to life and faith.

When God's time comes his grace will be irresistible and will overcome human ignorance, rebellion and unbelief. In this act the Holy Spirit re-creates and comes again continually to renew. "In this sense Jesus Christ is the hope even of these non-Christians."[18]

Thus the form of this coming as Spirit is that adapted to the time of the action between the first and second coming of Christ and related to our place in history. It is "his coming as the hope of all men"[19] in two distinctive and varied forms. It is the one Lord by the Spirit who comes, "his universally relevant coming in the Holy Spirit," that is, to the community; "and in the promise of the Holy Spirit,"[20] that is, to non-believers. Negatively, one can say that Christ is not now present as he was then in the resurrection or will be at the End yet it is the same Lord in the power of his exalted life in a different form. Positively, his absence in this way makes possible another form of his presence in the freedom, authority and grace of God, or, as Barth can also say, Christ's "own direct and personal coming."[21]

He is present in the full glory of the Mediator in the totality of his being and action. The older Protestant idea that his humanity remained in heaven but he came in the power of his deity is excluded. That dichotomy was a form of Nestorian dualism. Dualism is excluded by the very nature of the incarnation—God and man—the one Mediator. This again corresponds to the Easter event where he was not merely God but also human. The unity of God and humanity is not a revocable one. Christ always comes clothed in his humanity. A spirit which denied this would not be the Holy Spirit, and its presence would not be new life, would not be the Spirit of promise.

The particular form of the Spirit's presence in space, time and history is not limited by these. Its power is the power of Christ risen, absolute, undiminished and with no reserve. It is the power of Christ's prophetic office and as such is the real power of God unto salvation: "His promise is, then, in both its senses the work of God."[22] It is a *divine* work to be with the Church and move to its goal, It is also a *divine* work to claim and change people to become Christian. It is *God* who acts here by the Holy Spirit; to reject the Spirit is to turn one's back on God. There is no inadequacy in its presence and power but only in us. The second or middle form of the prophecy of Jesus Christ "is the total proclamation of the total love of God and the total salvation of man."[23] "There is repeated in it the anticipation of his final revelation. In it all things are already given to us and the world."[24] The work and presence of the Holy Spirit are thus eschatological throughout the course in powerfully glorious action and in the promise of future glory.

C. THE HOLY SPIRIT AND VOCATION

The whole of Christian faith and life is directly related to the Holy Spirit. Nowhere is this more obvious than in our calling (vocation) to be a Christian and to live the Christian life, for the Spirit is the active presence of Jesus Christ himself in the time between the ages, between the first and second coming. Barth expresses it like this: "The presence and action of the Holy Spirit are the *parousia* of Jesus Christ in the time between Easter and his final revelation."[25] In the perspective of Barth's *Church Dogmatics* this is an aspect of the prophetic office of Jesus Christ. The Lord as servant has reconciled the world to himself, altered the whole situation between himself and humanity, exalted us into permanent union with himself. This is his comprehensive, all-inclusive work of reconciliation. At the same time and in consequence he declares as prophet what he has done and carries this out in the power of the Holy Spirit. He does this in the present time and in so doing calls people to faith—to be Christians. Significantly Barth sees the call as being issued to all humanity on the basis of election which is the determination of all. All are in this sense predisposed by virtue of the reconciliation of all and not by any inherent capacity of humanity; but not all respond.

a) The Basis of Vocation.

The basis of vocation is God's election of grace in Jesus Christ "prior to its actualisation in his (humanity's) own history."[26] In this action directed *ad extra* to humanity God is at work not only as Son but also as Father and Holy Spirit, the triune God. Christ is thereto ordained by the Father and in obedience elects himself to be the God of sinful humanity. In so electing as the triune God the Holy Spirit maintains the unity of Father and Son. This is manifest in time in incarnation, reconciliation and the outpouring of the Spirit, and also in our vocation to faith. But its basis "is the prior history which precedes and underlies the event of vo-

cation in their own history,"[27] namely, the election of grace.
Rosato points out the significance of this basis when
he writes, "Reflection on the Spirits's unique function in the
divine election, however, allows Barth to attribute to the
Spirit's temporal mission a distinctive character. The Spirit
is to translate the divine calling of all men into the believer's personal experience of being called."[28] Because we are
all ontologically included in the election of grace a human
being is as such foreordained, foreknown, and predisposed
"for the work of the Holy Spirit to be accomplished in
him."[29] This is Barth's "point of contact", a predisposition
not in humanity's possibility but in the divine ordaining.
This, in its own way, is his answer to natural theology. It
does not exclude but alone makes possible each person's
particular calling. It is only this vocation that distinguishes
a Christian from a non-Christian. To be called is to know
and live by what has already been done on our behalf.

A serious question arises at this point in relation to
those who persist in unbelief. Barth seeks to answer it in
the following way: Human unbelief is objectively opposed
and countered in God's election and in reconciliation in
time. The thrust of God's grace by the Spirit is directed to
change the unbeliever into a believer. A person who remains in unbelief does so through his or her own fault, accepting as true what has already been declared false. Here
Barth wrestles with a problem which has baffled the minds
of theologians in all centuries, but does not find an answer
that is entirely satisfactory. However, the assertion of J.
Veitch[30] that, because of objective atonement, unbelief is
almost a form of faith—a *para*—faith as yet unrealised is
not true to Barth's position. Barth sees, rather, two aspects
that must be included in one's reckoning and thought—the
superabounding grace of God by the Spirit for our salvation, and the ugly reality of unbelief which contradicts but
cannot undo God's reconciliation. But because God has
chosen humanity from all eternity and in time reconciled us
to himself in Jesus Christ even the unbeliever stands in the
light of grace and in the promise of the Spirit. Veitch, however, correctly points to a dialectic in Barth's thought where

all are caught up in the economy of salvation as "potential recipients of the promise of the Spirit . . . . but because they have turned away from that light. . . the Gospel is still relevant to their sinful condition."[31]

b) The Event of Vocation.

Vocation is the power of Christ the Word operating by the Spirit directly and immediately in the fulness of his reconciling work in men and women. While Barth underlines the immediacy of the calling of men and women by the Word he also recognises mediacy in time and history through the testimony of the apostles and prophets in Holy Scripture and through the life and witness of the Church. Yet however we underline this aspect of it in our time between the ages, the emphasis is on Jesus Christ as the sole, active Subject contemporary with us and calling us by the Holy Spirit. Vocation, while temporal and historical, is essentially a spiritual act. Again it is clear—and Barth points this out—that the Holy Spirit is never the one who calls,[32] nor is the Spirit's action ever divorced from that of the Word as a kind of independent activity. The call of Christ goes out by Word and Spirit to an active recognition of his grace. This is "a spiritual process, because in it there can be no question of any other subject than the living Lord Jesus Christ acting immediately and directly in the power of his Word and by the Holy Spirit."[33]

But what happens to humanity in this process?[34] The one reconciling Christ addresses us by the Word of his grace in the power of the Spirit. It is the one single grace of the one whole Lord Jesus Christ addressed to the whole person by the one Holy Spirit. Again we see the strongly objective emphasis of Barth or, to put it otherwise, the subjective aspect of the Christian revelation related to the action of the Holy Spirit and not primarily to human response. For this reason Barth is critical of the older dogmatics' views on the *ordo salutis* (order of salvation) which organised the various aspects of our experience of grace in a certain order and sequence such as—calling, conversion, justification, mystical union, sanctification, assurance.[35] This Barth regards as putting the emphasis on hu-

man subjective experience—a successive, psychological
state or states rather than on the one act of God in his grace
in Christ by the Holy Spirit. It is true that many of these
terms are used in Scripture but, Barth argues, each represents the whole viewed from one particular angle and does
not present an ordered series or sequence.[36]

His critique of the *ordo salutis* can be summarised
as follows:

It makes a spiritual event a psychological and biographical description of the evolution of a Christian.

It is presented in such a multiplicity of forms that no
one could be exclusively followed as correct.

It weakens and devalues the terms themselves when
used in this way.

It turns what happens away from God's act in Christ
by the Holy Spirit to man, "to his Christian experiences and
states." [37] The end result is to centre attention on humanity
itself, the typical mistake which is manifest in some aspects
of Roman Catholicism, Liberal Protestantism and Evangelicalism.

On the contrary vocation focuses attention on God's
act in its totality and not on humanity's fragmented experiences of it. It is "the one total address to man of the living
Lord Jesus Christ" resulting not in "a progressive alteration" but in "his total alteration."[38] This does not mean that
a person is totally changed in a moment but that the whole
direction of one's life is by a total reconciliation in Christ
and – this word made effectual by the Spirit.

This can be described in two ways, as illumination,[39] and as awakening.[40] Illumination means that Christ
as the light of life, the power of his own reconciliation, ef-
fectually carries out his work in our lives: "Illumination
means that the light of life carries through its work in a particular man to its conclusion."[41] It is at one and the same
time Christ's work alone; this in turn enables it to be ours as
well. Or, in Barth's language, as a person is turned he "has
thus to turn himself from darkness to light ."[42] The sole
Subject makes humanity a secondary subject which it was
unable to be by itself. Again, no material addition is made

if it is described as awakening. This term, beloved of Pietism and Methodism, points to the analogue of the resurrection. It is a raising of the dead and not fanning into flame an inner spark. It is a new creation issuing in a total change. It points to the One who alone can do and does this, to Christ present in the power of the Spirit. This Barth shows as effective, leading to an active knowledge and the fruits of the Spirit: "We are dealing with the process which as his (Christ's) illumination is *effective revelation* and *active knowledge*, which is thus *fruitful illumination*, and which has thus to be described as awakening."[43] Awakening thus points both to the new creative and the dynamic nature of this action.

  c) The Goal of Vocation.

  The goal of vocation[44] is not simply the salvation of individuals, however true this is in itself, nor is it simply to add people to the Church—here Barth is critical of a mere nominal Christianity, a *Corpus Christianum*. Vocation has as its goal the raising up of Christians in union with Christ who will bear witness to the grace of Christ by the Spirit. If we think only of ourselves and our personal salvation we can end up in a holy (unholy) egoism. The Scripture forbids this and points to the dynamic of grace and reconciliation as embracing the world and pointing us back to Christ, to God that he may be all in all. Here again one finds the eschatological perspective, since Christians are themselves "the first-fruits of the prophetic work of Jesus Christ illumined and awakened by his Word in the power of the Holy Spirit."[45] They are in the world but not of it. They are called to obedient service and witness till he come. Barth puts the question to every Christian in a particularly personal way in relation to Paul's words of 1 Cor 9:16. 'Woe is me if I preach not the Gospel;" "Whether I like it or not, irrespective of who or what or how I am, whether I am worthy or unworthy, skilful or unskilful, am I forced to live for this Word and its declaration to all men?"[46] In the light of man's vocation the only proper Christian answer must be a glad affirmative.

D. COMMENTARY ON BARTH'S EXPOSITION

There are several distinctive features of Barth's theology which are evident in the above exposition. These may now be outlined.

a) In the first place his emphasis on the unity of mankind in God's action in reconciliation. Here there is a legitimate universalism following the biblical witness. On the one hand men and women are included in Christ's reconciliation but at the same time all are concluded as under God's righteous judgment and sentence of death. All have also the promise of the Spirit. On the other hand there is a very great difference between the Christian and the non-Christian since to the Christian the Spirit has come in effective power and this individual is on the way from one degree of faith to another towards the consummation. The movement of God by the Spirit has moved this person who has moved himself as a result and is on the way. For the other, the non-Christian, on the other hand, the same Spirit is also on the move, promised to a person but not yet illuminating and awakening the person to faith.

The criticism sometimes made of Barth that the distinction between the Christian and the non-Christian is simply one of "knowledge" in a purely intellectual sense is very far from the truth.[47] Barth himself points out that knowledge in the Bible is an intimate, personal, saving knowledge of Christ's reconciliation in the power of the Spirit. Not to know is to be outside this transforming experience. Again his emphasis on vocation as illumination and illumination as awakening to new life from the death of sin involving a new creation shows the falsity and misunderstanding underlying this criticism.

b) A further very important emphasis in this whole treatment is Barth's close association of Word and Spirit. The Word is Jesus Christ the Reconciler in his prophetic office present with us by the promised Spirit. It is clear from Barth's writings as a whole that Christ and Spirit are distinguished though one as divine in the eternal, triune being of God. Here the emphasis on the Word present by the Spirit points to their indissoluble unity in saving action. In this instance the Spirit is almost identical with Christ. This is an emphasis largely neglected in traditional pneumatology which tended to see the Spirit merely as the subjective side of God's revelation, the one by whom Christ is known. Here the Spirit is almost Christ's *Alter Ego*, his other self. The Spirit comes in Christ's absence or rather as Christ's new presence. The presence of the Spirit is the presence of Christ and each is that of the living presence of God with men and women.

Even when the Holy Spirit and Christ are not explicitly identified or correlated in the New Testament this relationship is implicit. It is Christ who lives in us and dwells in us just as the Holy Spirit does. However, the Spirit is never wholly identified with Christ nor does it supersede him nor act independently of him. Rather it makes him effective to us and within us, to conform us to the likeness of Christ.

H. Berkhof, while quoting Barth as representative of the more traditional view, points out that in this particular instance the Spirit as the presence of "the risen and mighty Lord" is an "insight. . . expressed in the last volumes of Barth's *Church Dogmatics*."[48] The Spirit is "no other than the presence and action of Jesus Christ himself: his stretched out arm; he himself in the power of his resurrection, i.e., in the power of his revelation as it begins in and with the power of his resurrection and continues its work from this point."[49] In this way the dynamic of Christ's prophetic Word works from him to us. "Christ as life-giving Spirit wants to take men into his fellowship in order that they may partake in and be transformed into the new humanity which he has obtained for us."[50]

c) The third strong emphasis here is on the Holy Spirit in relation to the eschaton. If Christ is the Eschatos and the Spirit is his reaching out in the present age to all in promise and as promised the Spirit is clearly also, by its presence now, the first-fruits and guarantee of ultimate redemption. The Holy Spirit is thus, in Barth's view, the sec-

ond form of Christ's parousia, his presence in the middle
form related both to what happened in reconciliation and
also already pointing to and anticipating the final revelation.

In the light of this it is therefore a peculiar misread-
ing of Barth's doctrine of the Spirit to say that it has a thrust
backwards but not forwards as do both R.W. Jenson and
Colin Gunton.[51] A proper reading and understanding of the
present eschatological perspectives as outlined in Barth's
later volumes make such a view quite impossible and incorrect. It is significant that Gunton bases his judgment on the
early passages in the *Church Dogmatics* 1/1. and writes,
"Any weakness in the discussion of the Holy Spirit will
militate against a satisfactory expression of the eschatological dimension of Christian theology, with the result that the
activity of God will tend to be located in the past rather
than in the present and future."[52] This is of course correct as
a statement but it is incorrect when applied to the theology
of Karl Barth. The above exposition as seen in his later volumes shows how wrong this view is, since the Spirit is the
power of Christ present today pointing to and in a sense
also realising now God's action in final redemption in the
future. Gunton does however admit that even in his earlier
writings present and future dimensions of the Spirit are not
entirely absent from Barth's *Church Dogmatics*.[53]

d) One of the strong emphases of Barth is the unity
of action of Christ by the Spirit. His aim in all this is to focus attention upon Christ, God's action in him and by him
in the Spirit rather than upon certain experiences which we
have as a result of Christ's action on us.

While not explicitly polemical his views are nevertheless at variance with those of others.

1) They differ from Roman Catholicism which so
divided up grace as to make it difficult to see it as the one
divine act of God for our salvation[54] Yet as Barth himself
points out, even Roman Catholics live and must live by the
one grace of Jesus Christ if they are to be Christian at all.[55]
Again—this one action of God in Christ by the Spirit excludes all repetition of his work and all attempts to take it

over as a human work of the Church.

2) They are written against Lutheran and other views of an *ordo salutis*; this is also meant to counter the view of various graces but more particularly it is meant to turn our gaze away from ourselves to Jesus Christ. This should not be thought as implying that Barth is unaware of the need for distinctive emphases like justification, sanctification and vocation. Rather it points to the totality of the one act of God in all these "moments" and sees each in the light of the whole.

3) They are an attempt to take up the genuine concerns of Pietism or in English speaking terms, Evangelicalism, which laid and lays great emphasis on conversion, regeneration, experience, life, holiness. Barth clearly regards these emphases as better than a merely nominal Christianity and as correct as far as they go, but he could not completely agree with the way they have generally been expressed in such circles. The subjective for him is not an independent theme in contradistinction to the objective as is the tendency in Pietism; it is but an aspect of the one revelation of God in Christ—what the Holy Spirit does in revelation. Otto Weber writes, "One sees here clearly how willing Barth is to take up and deal with the thinking and experiences of Pietism. But he does not do it uncritically. His understanding of vocation as a comprehensive act arms him against the idea that he must follow the other 'higher and better' way perhaps with the terms 'new birth' and 'conversion'. Not that he has anything against what is intended by 'regeneration' and 'conversion' but vocation which is really received and expresses itself in active knowledge embraces all human experiences."[56]

Barth's stress on the objectivity of God's action in Christ by the Holy Spirit makes him suspicious of what he regarded as humanity looking too much to itself, to his "experiences" of Christ, to "assurance" of salvation rather than to Christ himself. E. Busch speaks of this[57] as a form of Cartesianism where human thought revolves, primarily around itself and, even a religious person takes too much of a central place. Moreover Pietism had a strong sense of the individual whereas Barth gives greater place to the community as well as to the individual.

However, one should not end on an altogether negative note.[58] Not only did Barth take up the positive concerns of Pietists but he also could express a considerable measure of agreement with them on the following points: the necessity for witness by the person who experiences grace; the nature of grace as something outside of us which comes to us as objective; and the reality (in this light) of the depth of human sin. Despite the danger of centering attention on humanity (even religious humanity) in these statements, the positive side was that the individual became a witness to Jesus Christ and learned to rely solely upon his grace by the Holy Spirit.

At the same time the concern of Roman Catholicism to give humanity its place is taken up by Barth but in a quite different way. So is that of Lutheranism in its desire to point to the varied "moments" or "perspectives" in the one act of God in Christ by the Spirit.

NOTES

1. Cf. Charles Hodge, *Systematic Theology*, Vol. III, London and Edinburgh, 1873, Part IV, pp. 713-880; Heinrich Schmid, *Doctrinal Theology of the Evangelical Lutheran Church*, 3rd Edition, trs. Charles A. Hay and Henry E. Jacobs, Minneapolis, 1961, Part V. pp. 624-663.

2. A. Schweitzer, *The Quest of the Historical Jesus, From Reimarus to Wrede*, trs. W. Montgomery, London, 1910.

3. C. H. Dodd, *The Parables of the Kingdom*, London, 1936, passim.

4. Jürgen Moltmann, *Theology of Hope* (4), trs. James W. Leitch, London: S.C.M., 1974, passim.

5. Rudolf Bultmann. *Jesus Christ and Mythology*, London: S.C.M., 1960, passim; *History and Eschatology*, Edinburgh, 1955, pas-

sim. "New Testament and Mythology," in *Kerygma and Myth*, ed. Hans Werner Bartsch, trs. Reginald H. Fuller, London: S.P.C.K. 1953, Vol. 1. pp. 1-44.
6. See John Thompson, *Christ in Perspective in the Theology of Karl Barth*, pp. 126-135. Colm O'Grady, *The Church in the Theology of Karl Barth*, Vol. 1, London: Geoffrey Chapman, 1970, pp. 338 - 350.
7. *C.D.*, IV/3, 1. pp. 274ff.; see especially pp. 350f.
8. Ibid., p. 351.
9. Ibid., p. 351f.
10. Ibid., p. 351.
11. Ibid.
12. Ibid., p. 352.
13. Ibid., p. 353.
14. Ibid.
15. Ibid., p. 354.
16. Ibid.
17. Ibid., p. 355.
18. Ibid., p. 356.
19. Ibid.
20. Ibid.
21. Ibid. T. F. Torrance is critical of Barth's doctrine of creation which he says "did not offer an account of creation from an overarching trinitarian perspective", *How Karl Barth Changed My Mind*, p. 61. This is only very partially true, since, as we have seen, Barth definitely sets creation within a trinitarian context though possibly not a wholly overarching one.
22. Ibid., p. 358.
23. Ibid.
24. Ibid., p. 359.
25. *C.D.*, IV/3, 2, p. 503.
26. Ibid., p. 483.
27. Ibid., p. 484.
28. Rosato, op.cit., p. 85.
29. *C.D.*, IV/3, 2. p. 491.
30. J. A. Veitch, "Revelation and Religion in the Theology of Karl Barth," *S.J.T.*, XXIV, 1971, p. 19.
31. Ibid., p. 20.

32. *C.D.* IV/3, 2. p..503.

33. Ibid., pp. 501-502.

34. Ibid., pp. 504-505.

35. Ibid., p. 505f.

36. Ibid., p. 508.

37. Ibid., p. 507.

38. Ibid., pp. 507-508.

39. Ibid., pp. 508-511.

40. Ibid., pp. 511-514.

41. Ibid., p. 508.

42. Ibid., p. 509.

43. Ibid., p. 514; italics mine.

44. Ibid., p. 520ff.

45. Ibid., p. 557.

46. Ibid., p. 679.

47. Cf. Heinz Zahrnt, *The Question of God, Protestant Theology in the Twentieth Century*, trs. R. A. Wilson, London: Collins, 1969, pp. 115-116. He wrltes, "Believers and unbelievers are distinguished from one another by the fact that believers already possess knowledge of a given matter, which is still unknown to unbelievers, and consequently missionary activity consists in imparting this particular matter and making it known." (Ibid). He quotes the Swedish theologian Gustav Wingren as in substantial agreement with him (Ibid., p. 116). However, Bromiley gives a much more accurate statement when he comments, "Those who look to Barth for the odd idea that evangelism is merely informing people that they are saved are misinformed." G. W. Bromiley, *Introduction to the Theology of Karl Barth*, Edinburgh: T. & T. Clark, 1979, p. 203.

48. Hendrikus Berkhof, *The Doctrine of the Holy Spirit* Richmond, Virginia: John Knox Press, 1964, p. 29.

49. *C.D.*, IV/2, pp. 322-323.

50. Berkhof, op.cit., p. 27. Though less than Rosato, Berkhof leans towards a Spirit Christology which was never Barth's intention.

51. Colin E. Gunton, *Becoming and Being, The Doctrine of God in Charles Hartsborne and Karl Barth*, OUP, 1978, pp. 163-166. Gunton quotes R. W. Jenson's views in *God after God* pp. 173ff. as similar to his own.

52. Gunton, ibid., p. 163.

53. Ibid., pp. 164-165.

54. *C.D.*, IV/1, pp. 84-88; cf. Rudolf Ehrlich, op.cit., p. 106-112.

55. Ibid., p. 88 for a discussion of Barth's views. Barth writes, "But we must not omit an irenical and ecumenical word. . . There is a very deep peace (beyond any understanding) between us Evangelical Christians and our Catholic fellow-Christians who are badly instructed in this doctrine. We cannot believe that they do in fact live by the grace which is so dreadfully divided in their dogmatics. Rather, we have to believe, and it is comforting to believe, that they as well as we—if only we did it better—do live by the one individual grace of Jesus Christ." (Ibid.). Gerhard von Rad in his commentary on Genesis I, trs. John H. Marks, London: S.C.M. 1961, pp 57-58 indicates in a way close to Barth that the text speaks less of the nature than of the purpose of the image. Further, male and female show a being for another in a community which reflects the being of the triune God.

56. Weber, *Karl Barths Kirchliche Dogmatik*, p. 311.

57. Eberhard Busch, *Karl Barth und die Pietisten*, Die Pietismuskritik des jungen Karl Barth und ihre Erwiderung, Munich: Chr. Kaiser Verlag, 1978, p. 296. (Karl Barth and Pietism: its critique by the younger Barth and a reply).

58. Busch, Ibid., pp. 300-303.

CHAPTER ELEVEN

THE SPIRIT AS LORD

EVAULATION AND CRITIQUE OF P. J. ROSATO'S BOOK

In the previous chapters we have from time to time quoted P. J. Rosato's interpretation of Barth both with approval and with reservations. After summarising Barth, Rosato goes on to offer what he calls "improvisations",[1] that is, improvements on Barth's pneumatology. But improvements imply weaknesses or even wrong views and Rosato, while indicating Barth's greatness, clearly distances himself from him in a variety of ways. In fact the last two chapters of his book read like a summation of most of the criticisms of Barth made over many years but related now specifically to pneumatology.

We take up these as Rosato does in two ways, (A) the actual objections he raises to Barth and (B) his own alternative reconstruction.

A. CRITIQUE OF BARTH'S VIEWS

Rosato's areas of disagreement with Barth he summarises as the trinitarian, anthropological and ontological dimensions of Barth's Spirit theology. The common theme of all these, as it is the general criticism of Roman Catholicism and Neo-Protestantism, is that in Barth's *Church Dogmatics* humanity is downgraded at the expense of God. Creation and nature are in danger of being undervalued because of this form of Spirit theology. The question that Rosato poses and answers in the affirmative is: can human au-

tonomy and freedom co-exist and co-operate with the freedom and reality of the Holy Spirit?

a) Trinitarian Aspects

The trinitarian aspects of Barth's Spirit theology
over-shadow humanity's role in history. Barth is said to
have such a strict formalistic and speculative trinitarian
view of God and the Spirit [2] that God is divorced from history, from humanity and from its social and political life. If
the conception of the Trinity is remote and abstract so also
is that of the Spirit. Rosato accuses Barth of a Spirit theology so overemphasised as to neglect the role of humanity.

The formalism which he sees in Barth's theology of
the Trinity destroys Barth's attempt at dynamism and actualism in his theology. It also means that Barth's trinitarian
pneumatology does not leave room for humans to co-
operate with the Spirit. The reason for this is a Western
scholastic framework for the Trinity which lacks dynamism
whereas the East, which Rosato favours, provides this. But
he is well aware of the fact that Barth and Eastern thought
have many striking parallels and similarities. The main difference is that the Eastern view respects human independence and shows humanity as having a mediating function
in history. Basically it is Barth's preference for a christological concentration that lends his trinitarian view its formalism. The Spirit has thus a merely noetic function. Instead
one should see the Spirit as the opening of Father and Son
to human history. There is in Barth no interaction between
God's Spirit and human nature—the Spirit's internal action
in the Trinity predominates. Hence the human role is under-
played; humanity which can induce God's self-revelation
and play a mediating role is excluded. Moreover, the back-
ward-pointing aspect of the Spirit is so emphasised that
there is little forward-pointing role. The Spirit points back
to its role in the Trinity rather than forward to its work in
the world. To put it in another way, the originative Trinity
in which the Spirit plays this role takes a predominant place
and the eschatological Trinity plays a minor role.

In response one can make the following points:

1. Barth's early trinitarian doctrine has indeed with

some truth been accused of a measure of formalism.[3] This aspect, however, became less apparent as Barth anchored it more in the reality of reconciliation and related the Trinity to the cross. It is in the cross and resurrection of Christ, in the utmost humiliation and contradiction of it, overcome and transcended in the resurrection, that one sees God as Father sending the Son and the Son suffering, and, as a result of his death and resurrection, sending the Holy Spirit. In Barth's later more mature theology the Trinity is distinctly related to the historical work of our salvation and loses its formal nature.

It is not merely a matter of the Spirit pointing back with a role only in the immanent Trinity. Who God is in himself is seen in the economy of salvation by the power of the Spirit. It is in fact quite the opposite of a monologue in heaven—as it is sometimes put.[4] Rosato fails to take account of the positive answers given to Barth's critics by writers like Hübner[5] and Schlichting.[6]

2. Rosato's view deals with a particular and questionable conception of human nature, autonomy and freedom. This conceives humanity as reaching up to, seeking after God, in dialogue with him, and responding to him, so that while God is said to be sovereign and transcendent there is a form of mutual reciprocity. Here there is a failure to consider with Anselm the seriousness and the weight of human sin—something that Rosato very rarely discusses at all. Here too is the essence of the Reformation objection to Catholicism—that it gives humanity too great a place, sees it co-operating with grace and so endangering the *sola gratia*. Barth's insights are more correct; he sees humanity in reaching up to the divine by its sinfulness fashioning images and false gods of its own conception and imagining and so deceiving itself. Again Rosato seems to have taken no account of this strain in Barth's thought.

3. Rosato has been strongly influenced by Moltmann's view of the Trinity[7] which sees God as originative Trinity working through human history and reaching a real fulfilment in a so called eschatological Trinity. But are there two Trinities and does the Spirit and so God only real-

ly come to itself and its glory at the end? This certainly seems to be the implication of Moltmann's and Rosato's views. In other words here is indeed a very questionable view of the Trinity. Moreover, it is quite mistaken to say that Barth's view of the Spirit simply points backwards. Too little attention has been paid, in this as in other works, to Barth's last volumes where the Spirit is the power of the eschaton and not merely of the centre. The Spirit, as we have seen, is Christ himself in the power of the resurrection as the Lord of all, embracing the totality of humanity and the cosmos and acting in it, moving us towards the end, and so bringing about and being that end. In Barth's later theology the Spirit does not simply point back to Christ but with him points forward and acts in a way which has real significance now and for the future. It has a missionary and eschatological reach in one, since Christ in reconciliation includes and embraces the whole cosmos.

Not only therefore does Rosato misinterpret Barth but his own "improvement" is an unacceptable alternative, a theologically untenable trinitarian doctrine.

b) Anthropology

According to Rosato the anthropological aspect overshadows our God-given autonomy. Humanity's being is a being in relation and so it has only reality by continually renewed encounters with the Spirit. A question mark is thus placed against human individuality and subjectivity; our being in its relative independence is subordinated to our being in grace; there is thus a docetic tendency in Barth's theology. This is essentially the same objection to Barth as that of A. B. Come[8] and George Hendry.[9] Can one on this view be free either to believe or to reject grace?

Another way of putting this is that Barth's pneumatic anthropology is monistic, that is, in danger of so exalting the Spirit that our spiritual nature is virtually erased. Not only is there christomonism, there is, for Rosato, a pneumatomonism. Rosato wishes to give priority to the Spirit to avoid a too great emphasis on humanity but at the same time he wishes to accord him a greater place, freedom and spiritual nature than he believes Barth does. Rosato traces back the supposed disorder to Barth's ontology, that is the view that apart from an "ontological connection to Jesus Christ man has no natural relationship to God."[10] For Rosato the first article of the Creed, belief in God the Father, must be seen to some extent apart from the second, belief in Jesus Christ. Summarizing one could say that Barth's view of humanity and pneumatology is determined by his christology which means that the Spirit who makes us human is always tied to Christ and is never free to give us a real measure of independence. Likewise our being in relation is exclusively tied up with that of the man Christ Jesus.

Rosato argues further that Barth himself gives an example in the Spirit-filled Jesus of a man open to God. Here is a model suitable to the reciprocity or complementarity of nature and grace—Jesus as the Lord and also as the human responsive to the Spirit. Here we have an "anthropology from the Spirit" which grants both the vertical perspective of the Spirit's primacy and the horizontal perspective of our native spirituality their full worth and independence.[11]

Rosato wants a dialogical relationship between the transcendent Spirit and humanity's graced but autonomous freedom and spirit. In this sense humanity co-operates in its redemption. For Barth on the contrary "the Spirit is seen exclusively as the one sent from Christ, but not inclusively as the one leading all things to the glory of the end-time through the mediation of mankind's secular experiments."[12] Here the main criticism of Barth is that the Spirit is too closely linked to Christ; it should be seen also as the Spirit of the Father and as the Spirit at work in the whole of the universe apart from Christ.

To this section the following response can be made.

1. Rosato's view of autonomous humanity must be challenged along with his criticism that Barth fails to recognise and respect human freedom. Stuart McLean answers Come[13] and so Rosato by pointing to the different ways the Spirit is related to the whole person and the distinction Barth makes between creation and providence on the one hand and redemption on the other. In the former humanity

is affirmed in its significance as fully human where "the ordinary meaning of freedom's choice among options, or freedom as self-determination, is affirmed."[14] McLean points to
the distinction between the *functions* of the Spirit in redemption and creation; in the former humanity is brought
into a saving relationship in its whole being with God, in
the latter the function of the Spirit applies to all creatures.
The distinction between Barth and Rosato here is that for
Barth this is intimately related to and known only through
God's covenant fulfilled in reconciliation, whereas for Rosato it has a semi-independent role. Rosato tends to isolate
creation from redemption in an unacceptable way whereas
Barth relates and co-ordinates them.

    2. The question of humanity graced and so co-
operating freely with grace raises an issue where there is a
subtle but real difference between Barth and Reformation
theology on the one hand and Catholicism on the other.
Both are concerned to say that all is of grace. But with the
Reformers Barth says that it is of grace in such a way that
humanity does not co-operate in its own salvation at any
stage. Even to speak of prevenient grace does not mean
this. All is of God who enables us and gives us through
faith our true humanity. Rosato says with the Roman Catholic tradition—yes, but. In making it all of grace God enables humanity to act in such a way that it is to some extent
autonomous and so co-operates in its redemption. While
Barth believes that humanity is, under grace, the subject of
reconciliation, he rightly sees this view of Rosato's as giving us a contributory share in our own salvation which is
unacceptable, however meagre it is meant to be. In fact it
does not exalt the freedom of humanity but gives it an autonomy which threatens grace. The answer which Barth
gives in Volume IV/2 of the *Church Dogmatics* shows
clearly that it is as humanity is set free by the Spirit that it
is a true subject and truly human.

    3. In questioning the place of the Spirit in Barth out-
side the Church Rosato touches on a crucial issue in Barth's
theology or rather he fails to mention it at all. Barth's answer would, I believe, be the perfectly legitimate one that

he gives in the *Church Dogmatics* Volume IV/3 on
"Truths" and "Lights" *extra muros ecclesiae*—outside the
walls of the Church.[15] Since by reconciliation Christ is Lord
of all and embraces all in his prophetic work he is also active and alive by the Spirit outside the Church in the world.
Yet this presence and Spirit cannot be different from but is
the same manifest in reconciliation—the Spirit of the Father and the Son and not simply the Spirit of the Father
alone. In other words the Spirit in the world and his activities cannot contradict but rather confirm him as the Spirit of
Christ and so the Spirit of God.

The Spirit is always the Spirit of Christ wherever
and however found; it is not a matter of the Spirit in the
world adding a new dimension to God's activity beyond
revelation or apart from it but unfolding and confirming it.
This does not exclude but includes the parousia and eschatology.

Rosato gives no exposition of this fruitful area of
Barth's thought. Indeed it has been generally neglected.

c) Reason and Ontology

Rosato's third objection to Barth's theology is that
his pneumatology replaces human reason.[16] "The pneumatic
mediation of truth which dominates the *Church Dogmatics*
makes the free search of human reason irrelevant"[17]—and
natural theology unnecessary and wrong. There is no rational criterion of previously held belief in God by which to
judge the validity of the Christian claims. According to Rosato the Christian revelation and natural knowledge of God
are identical. The Spirit is at work in human reason apart
from the Word. Arguing in a way reminiscent of Thomas
Aquinas, Rosato states that from faith in God one can then
argue to a general philosophical notion of God. One can
then go on in this light to speak of faith in intelligible
terms. In other words an alliance between faith and reason
is possible and necessary. Without this, he argues, one ends
in subjectivism, for it is only as the Spirit and human reason meet in dialogue that truth emerges. Truth is not tied to
the Christ event but by the Spirit and reason is known both
before and after Christ. Jesus Christ, in this sense, is not the

ontological basis and content of the truth but beside him there is a general ontological principle which is rooted in our created nature. The Spirit in human reason must be allowed to go beyond the Word and itself to have ontic power and validity.

One can put this otherwise by saying that the Spirit should be freed from the purely noetic function of teaching Christ to accomplish "new realisations of divine truth among men."[18] In one sense Jesus is the truth, but in another, needs the "ontic reinforcement" of the Spirit. Because a person is a being created by God faith must and can be allied to an ontology of being, that is, it must ascribe "an autonomous ontological structure to man himself"[19] analogous to God's being—an *analogia entis*.

In response to this criticism one may answer in the following way:

1. Rosato seems to make the assumption that human reason is the place of entry of Spirit and that humanity by the Spirit in its reason can respond to and know God apart from revelation. He has however given little attention to the question of the nature of Barth's doctrine of reconciliation which reveals both God's grace and human impotence. Is not reason tainted with the same stubborn opposition to God as all other faculties and can it then be the point of contact, the upward reach to God, Rosato assumes? It is impossible, as Barth points out, to have an identity between our conception of God and God's own Word by the Spirit about himself. But, taught by Word and Spirit, the reason can be re-directed to understand and give an account of revelation. If one does not speak of an alliance between faith and reason in the ordinary sense, this does not mean that faith is irrational but rather follows the rationality contained within the Word itself and seeks to interpret it.

2.) Is there not a serious danger here of separating Word and Spirit in a way that is unknown to the New Testament? The Spirit is always the Spirit of the Word since Jesus Christ is the Lord of all, even if this understanding is unknown in the world. Does the revelation of God in Christ need to be supplemented by the Spirit working in the world in general apart from Christ? Is Christ then not the Lord of all and is not the Holy Spirit always his Spirit?

3. Can one have this mixo-philosophical-theological view which, while attempting to retain the uniqueness of the Christ event, yet sets beside it a rival criterion of truth? This is a serious and a highly debatable area and Barth's position is at least as tenable as that of those who oppose it.

In general it can be said that in his writing Rosato separates the Spirit as the Creator Spirit from the Redeemer Spirit—the former acting directly on humanity and its reason, the latter acting through Christ. Barth, however, has given a better model of the relation of grace to nature in covenant and reconciliation as the basis of creation and has shown their intimate relationship and inter-dependence.

At the same time Rosato points to what he sees as a paradox in Barth's thought. The Spirit not only dominates the human and minimizes its role but it is itself subjected to an overriding, predominant christology.[20] In the former the Spirit restricts the human role and gives it little independent function; in the latter it points back to Christ but not forwards to new achievements in history. These points have already been dealt with so we will restrict ourselves here to an examination of Rosato's alternative proposal—a christology in a pneumatic framework.

B. ROSATO'S RECONSTRUCTION

There are, according to Rosato, two serious weaknesses in Barth's pneumatology, namely, a lack of emphasis on the Spirit's ontic role and on human mediation. Rosato claims, moreover, that in the doctrines of the Virgin Birth and Jesus' humanity we have examples of a Spirit christology in Barth's *Church Dogmatics*.[21] He feels that had Barth developed this further his whole theology would have benefited. However, as things stand, Rosato accuses Barth of a too strong Logos christology "from above" as a reaction to Neo-Protestant reductionism. However, one must point out that Barth's theology is not merely a logos christology from above; it is a christology of reconciliation based on God's action in Christ which is both from above to below and at the same time from below to above, and centered on the crucified and risen Lord Jesus Christ.

The question that one must ask of Rosato is this: is not a Spirit christology simply a return to the old heresy of Adoptionism? Rosato argues that there is both a valid and an invalid form of adoptionism. The latter views Jesus simply as a Spirit-filled man; the former seeks to show how Jesus' pre-existence can be preserved (and so his divinity) "through an affirmation of the singular indwelling of the eternal Spirit in him."[22] Rosato clearly wants to maintain the divinity of Jesus Christ, his consubstantial union with the Father. The question is, can a revitalised pneuma christology do this and how? Rosato argues that the framework of the Scriptures provides such a christology with the concept of Spirit overarching prophets, Christ and Church. But in what way is Jesus unique since others are filled with the Spirit too? He answers, "In this absolutely single case Jesus is led so fully into the being of God that his reciprocal dialogue with the Father constitutes him as God's Son from the very moment of his existence."[23] But where and when does Jesus' existence begin—with the eternal Father as eternal Son or with his birth or at the beginning of his public ministry? Rosato wants to affirm the first; his theological basis means one of the others—in fact a denial of Jesus' divinity. His model of a pneuma—sarx christology is not an improvement on the Logos—sarx tradition. Traditional christology states that the eternal Logos or Son of God entered our humanity by the agency of the Holy Spirit through the Virgin Mary, fashioning a human form and uniting it with himself—truly God and truly man. A Spirit christology tries to say that since the Spirit is divine it is connected with Jesus not just functionally but ontologically, that is, the divine Being is present in Jesus and makes him one with the Father. This however does not affirm Jesus' divinity nor can it.

Rosato varies his theme slightly by stating[24] that in its search for justice and freedom the Christian community

claims that in Jesus a Spirit-filled man by giving himself
for such righteousness and liberation was vindicated by the
Father raising him from the dead. From the beginning of
his mission Jesus, filled with the Spirit, was one with the
Father and "his resurrection reveals that he is one with the
very being of the Father."[25] This last statement is true but
cannot be reached from Rosato's premises. Rosato believes
that Jesus' ontic being (divinity) is to be considered after an
examination of his singular Spirit-filled historical function.
The Spirit is at work everywhere beyond Christ allowing
not only the original creation of the Father and recreation
by the God-man but "transcreation" in the socio-political
realm.[26] The Spirit acts in the pattern supplied by Jesus but
not in an exclusively Christocentric way as with Barth.

But, as we have seen above, Rosato's form of christology cannot render what it desires—a theology orientated
to the present needs of humanity beginning with the history
of Jesus and leading on to manifest his union with God.
The most it can do is to show Jesus as singularly filled with
the Spirit whether at birth or at the beginning of his mission
but scarcely as the eternal Son of God. Nor can Rosato's
emphasis on the resurrection make Jesus anything more
than man divinely filled and led; it cannot yield what logos
christology does—an eternally divine Son uniting himself
with us for us and for our salvation. Here in fact the second
form of adoptionism is as invalid as the first. Rosato ends
with what the Germans call a"Jesuology" and not a proper
christology.

It is clear that if one begins with a Spirit-christology
as Rosato does, one must come to a negative conclusion on
Barth's pneumatology and that of the Christian tradition as
a whole. Further, Rosato must end up with a highly dubious
conception of the Trinity—a triune God who is only completed through his involvement with us—a view similar to
that of Moltmann.

At the end Rosato admits that his own critique of
Barth "may indeed make God's divine pneuma seem to be a
bit poor"[27] and so indeed it does.

C. CONCLUSIONS

The above discussions have led to the following conclusions in relation to Barth's thoughts in general and to pneumatology in particular.

1. There is the clear impression of the spiritual quality and power of the writing combined with concentrated thought on the content of theology. In this sense the Spirit is the power enabling us to see and think aright about God revealed in Jesus Christ and witnessed to in the Scriptures. One does not and cannot pursue theology in a vacuum or as a purely academic study but as an act of worship which follows the mode of thought the Scriptures themselves prescribe. Rosato finds in Barth one who uses Schleiermacher's form (methodology) to a large extent. Barth would claim that if this is so this is part of the continuing fascination Schleiermacher had for him since, almost unconsciously, he (Schleiermacher) followed the biblical thought-form —though giving it a quite different content from Barth.

2. The second main impression is of a very strong unitary view in Barth's whole theology. This is not a "system" imposed from without to which theology conforms but one which the biblical testimony itself requires and implies. God is one in his being and action but is at the same time the eternally rich (*ewig reich*) God; varied in his ways yet one. This unitary view, corresponding to the nature of God with its rich variety, is seen in the total scope and range of Barth's theology. It embraces the being and action of God as triune, his one act and will in election, his one act in revelation and reconciliation, his one grace in calling sinners to faith in himself in the context of the believing community and his one word of witness to and in the world. In each one can envisage and have the whole and a great variety of moments or emphases. But in each and all it is the one triune God active in making himself known to us and powerfully present on our behalf. If the Holy Spirit is the means of all this reaching us the end product is both faith in and testimony to Jesus Christ to the glory of the triune God.

3. A further emphasis which has emerged from this study is a confirmation of the christological starting point and concentration of all Barth's theology. This is in contrast and opposed to Rosato who tends to give a priority to pneumatology but is also at times ambivalent and unsure on this point. Barth, on the contrary, maintains throughout his christological starting point which leads from and to the trinity, election, reconciliation, pneumatology, ecclesiology and a social and political concern. It is correct to say, as Rosato does, that the Holy Spirit plays the mediating role between Christ and us, but wrong to infer from this that pneumatology is virtually Barth's main concern.

The clear impression a study of the doctrine of the Spirit makes is that it is integrated by means of christology into the structure of Barth's total perspective, a perspective, moreover, which cannot be understood apart from the various aspects of it.

Further, the action of the triune God is one directed by God's eternal choice and will to be our God – for us and for our salvation. This movement is downwards and outwards in reconciling, renewing power, testifying to the world who God is, what he has done and is doing. It is the Holy Spirit who has the indispensable role of making this known to us and real in us but it is the Spirit in this set of relationships. This divine movement to us and in us is at the same time one to the whole of humanity and to the whole of life in its social, political and cosmic perspectives. There is no area where God is not sovereign, where Jesus Christ is not King, and where the Holy Spirit is not Lord.

4. Another aspect of Barth's thought is the emphasis (particularly in his later works) on God in Christ present directly and personally and active by the Holy Spirit. The purpose of this is to let God be God and to manifest his grace and his reconciling action in us. It is to show the freedom, Lordship and immediacy of God. It is to prevent anything from coming between Jesus Christ and us. It is to maintain that the sole mediation is by the Holy Spirit. It is particularly noticeable in the prophetic Word of Jesus Christ who, having reconciled us and the world to God,

speaks the Word of this reconciling work immediately to humanity.

In this way Barth gives less place to human mediation than traditional Reformation thought and at times leaves the impression that mediation of others is almost set aside. This is indeed a problematic area in his later theology. It seems, however, to be untrue to his general position (save in the case of the sacraments) for Bible, Church, and confessions all play their part and are used by God to speak directly to us.

NOTES

1. Rosato, *The Spirit as Lord*, pp. 131ff.

2. Ibid., p. 135f.

3. Eberhard Jüngel, *God As The Mystery of the World*, points out that Barth's earlier trinitarian structure has a formal character based on "God reveals himself as the Lord." This is, however, corrected and avoided in the later volumes of the *Church Dogmatics* by a strong emphasis on the humanity of Jesus in reconciliation.

4. Heinz Zahrnt, *The Question of God*, trs. R. A. Wilson, London: Collins, 1976, pp. 112ff.

5. E. Hübner, "Monolog im Himmel" Zur Barth-Interpretation von Heinz Zahrnt, *Evangelische Theologie*, No. 31, II, 1971, pp. 63-86.

6. Wolfhart Schlichting, *Biblische Denkform in der Dogmatik*, Zürich: Theologischer Verlag, pp . 185 ff .

7. Rosato, op.cit., p. 135; cf. Moltmann, *The Church in the Power of the Spirit*, pp. 50ff.

8. A. B. Come, *An Introduction to Barth's "Dogmatics" for Preachers*, Philadelphia: Westminster Press, 1963, p. 152.

9. George S. Hendry, *The Holy Spirit in Christian Theology*, London: S.C.M., 1965, pp. 110ff. The question of Barth and human autonomy is more fully discussed by John Macken, *The Autonomy Theme in the Theology of Karl Barth, Church Dogmatics: Karl Barth and his Critics*. Cambridge University Press, 1990. Contrary to many interpreters of Barth, Macken seeks to show that Barth provides a posi-

tive account of human autonomy especially as his theology developed
in his later writings.

10. Rosato, op.cit., p. 143.

11. Ibid., p. 145.

12. Ibid., p. 148.

13. Stuart McLean, *Humanity in the Thought of Karl Barth*,
Edinburgh: T. & T. Clark, 1981, pp. 60 and 65 n. 15.

14. Ibid., p. 45.

15. *C.D.*, IV/3,1, pp. 110ff; see for a summary, John Thompson, *Christ in Perspective*, pp. 114ff. See also Jüngel, *The Doctrine of
the Trinity*, pp.

16. Rosato, op.cit., p. 149.

17. Ibid.

18. Ibid., p. 152.

19. Ibid., p. 154.

20. Ibid., pp. 157ff.

21. Ibid., p. 173.

22. Ibid., p. 175.

23. Ibid., p. 176.

24. Ibid., p. 178.

25. Ibid.

26. Ibid., p. 179

27. Ibid., p. 187.

DATE DUE